# Women's Books of Hours in Medieval England

**Library of Medieval Women** **ISSN 1369–9652**

Series Editor: Jane Chance

The Library of Medieval Women aims to make available, in an English translation, significant works by, for, and about medieval women, from the age of the Church Fathers to the sixteenth century. The series encompasses many forms of writing, from poetry, visions, biography and autobiography, and letters to sermons, treatises and encyclopedias; the subject matter is equally diverse: theology and mysticism, classical mythology, medicine and science, history, hagiography, and instructions for anchoresses. Each text is presented with an introduction setting the material in context and a guide to further reading.

We welcome suggestions for future titles in the series. Proposals or queries may be sent directly to the editor or publisher at the addresses given below; all submissions will receive prompt and informed consideration.

Professor Jane Chance. E-mail: jchance@rice.edu

Boydell & Brewer Limited, PO Box 9, Woodbridge, Suffolk, IP12 3DF, UK. E-mail: boydell@boydell.co.uk. Website: www.boydell.co.uk

**Previously published titles in this series appear at the back of this book**

# Women's Books of Hours in Medieval England

## Selected Texts Translated from Latin, Anglo-Norman French and Middle English with Introduction and Interpretive Essay

Charity Scott-Stokes
Clare Hall, Cambridge

D. S. BREWER

First published 2006
D. S. Brewer, Cambridge

Reprinted in paperback and transferred to digital printing 2012

ISBN 978–1–84384–070–1 hardback
ISBN 978–1–84384–300–9 paperback

D. S. Brewer is an imprint of Boydell & Brewer Ltd
PO Box 9, Woodbridge, Suffolk IP12 3DF, UK
and of Boydell & Brewer Inc.
668 Mount Hope Ave, Rochester, NY 14620-2731, USA
website: www.boydellandbrewer.com

A CIP catalogue record for this book is available
from the British Library

This publication is printed on acid-free paper

Typeset by Pru Harrison, Hacheston, Suffolk

# Contents

## Illustrations

**for Natascha and Sebastian**

# Acknowledgements

I would like to acknowledge the generous help I have received in the many libraries I have visited, and especially from the staff of the manuscripts department at Cambridge University Library. Bristol City Council, the Syndics of Cambridge University Library and the Trustees of the Cranston Library, Reigate, kindly helped with photography, and gave permission for photographs from their manuscripts to be printed. I thank the following institutions and individuals for kind permission to print translations from manuscripts in their keeping: the Trustees of the Blackburn Museum and Art Gallery, the Boston Public Library / Rare Books Department, Bristol City Council, the Fitzwilliam Museum in Cambridge, the Syndics of Cambridge University Library, Exeter University Library and the Abbess and Sisters of Syon Abbey, the Keeper of the Brotherton Collection at Leeds University Library, the British Library, London, the Pierpont Morgan Library, New York, the Norfolk Museums & Archaeology Service, the Stadtbibliothek in Nuremberg, Germany, the Keeper of Special Collections and Western Manuscripts at the Bodleian Library, Oxford, the Trustees of the Cranston Library, Reigate, the University of Illinois Library at Urbana-Champaign, and the Dean and Chapter of York.

I am grateful to Jocelyn Wogan-Browne for useful comments on an early draft of some of the translations, to Natascha Scott-Stokes for extensive help with the introduction, interpretive essay and glossary, and to the publisher's reader for careful and helpful comments and suggestions throughout.

Somerville College, Oxford, provided a travel bursary which enabled me to visit libraries in Illinois and New York. Sebastian Meier-Ewert enabled me to visit Boston. The Modern Humanities Research Association provided a grant towards the costs of publication. My thanks to all of them.

**Printed and published with the assistance of the Modern Humanities Research Association**

## Abbreviations

| | |
|---|---|
| *AH* | *Analecta Hymnica Medii Aevi*. Ed. G.M. Dreves and C. Blume, with H.M Bannister. 1886–1922. Leipzig: O.R. Reisland. |
| EETS | Early English Text Society; O.S. Original Series; E.S. Extra Series. |
| *IMEP* | *The Index of Printed Middle English Prose*. Ed. R.E. Lewis, N.F. Blake, and A.S.G. Edwards. 1985. New York & London: Garland. |
| *IMEV* | *The Index of Middle English Verse*. Ed. C. Brown and R.H. Robbins. 1943. New York: Columbia University Press. |
| *IMEV* Suppl. | *Supplement to the Index of Middle English Verse*. Ed. R.H. Robbins and J.L. Cutler. 1965. Lexington: University of Kentucky Press. |
| *MMBL* | *Medieval Manuscripts in British Libraries*. Vols 1–3, N.R. Ker; Vol. 4, N.R. Ker and A.J. Piper. 1969–92. Oxford: Clarendon Press. |
| *RH* | *Repertorium Hymnologicum. Catalogue des chants, hymnes, proses, séquences, tropes en usage dans l'Eglise latine depuis les origines jusqu'à nos jours*, I–VI. U. Chevalier. 1892–1920. Louvain–Brussels: Société des Bollandistes. |
| *Roman Breviary* | *The Roman Breviary*. An English Version: compiled by the Benedictine Nuns of the Abbey of Our Lady of Consolation, at Stanbrook in Worcestershire. Ed. C.F. Brown. 1936. London: Burns, Oates & Washbourne. |

# Preface

The book of hours is said to have been the most popular book owned by the laity in the later Middle Ages. The earliest surviving exemplar made in England was designed and illustrated by William de Brailes in Oxford in the mid-thirteenth century, for an unknown young lady whom he portrayed in the book several times. Women were often patrons or owners of such books, which were usually illustrated. It is clear from manuscript catalogues, and from authoritative studies such as those by Janet Backhouse, John Harthan and Roger Wieck, that the majority of the surviving medieval books of hours were made and used in continental Europe. Yet some were made in England, or for use in England, and of these at least fifty can be positively identified as having been made for a woman patron, or having been in female ownership at an early date.

This volume brings together a selection of texts in translation from women's books of hours. The texts are of great importance to a Library of Medieval Women, since they are fundamental to an understanding of medieval piety, and women book owners recited them regularly. Although some do actually still occur in bibles or prayer-books, others have to be sought in specialist publications, often embedded in other material, and a few have not until now been available at all in modern editions or translations.

Most of the manuscripts considered here are now located in British libraries. One is in Germany. Manuscripts from Boston, New York, and Urbana-Champaign in Illinois provide only a representative sampling of books of hours in American collections. A full investigation of American libraries would undoubtedly yield further manuscripts of great interest and relevance to this field of study.

The book is intended for the general reader, as well as for students of medieval literature, social and religious history, cultural studies and women's studies, at undergraduate or postgraduate level. The glossary and annotated bibliography will facilitate access to these materials for readers who are not familiar with Christian traditions or terminology.

1. The Annunciation, from Isabel Ruddok's Hours. Bristol Public Library MS 14, fol. 14v

# Introduction

## Background, Development and Contents of the Book of Hours

A medieval book of hours was in essence a miscellany of prayers, made for an individual, a family or a community. It was designed for use at home, and also, in some instances, at church. It was intended primarily for private devotion, that is, as a book enabling its users to direct their minds in faithful service to the worship of God in private prayer during the course of their daily lives. There was also a strong focus on the Blessed Virgin Mary. It was in the main a religious compilation, yet it could also include secular, or worldly, items. The manuscripts were often beautifully illustrated, sometimes with embroidered or bejewelled covers, and even bags to keep them in – valuable, holy and protective in their material substance as well as in the prayers enclosed.

This introduction offers background information designed to put the book of hours in context, followed by discussion of the standard and supplementary textual contents, the visual aspect and music, and some observations on the original languages of the texts.

*

Since the Virgin Mary features very prominently in the book of hours, and the core text of the book is the Little Office, or Hours, of the Blessed Virgin (text **1**),[1] it is useful to review the growth of narratives and veneration of Mary from the early centuries of Christianity to the late Middle Ages.

Mary is the central figure in the New Testament narrative of events in Nazareth and Bethlehem leading up to the Nativity of Jesus, as recounted most fully in the gospel of St Luke. She received the salutation of the angel Gabriel at the Annunciation, conceived and gave birth to Jesus, and nursed the child as the shepherds and Magi, or three kings,

[1] The term ‘book of hours’ is a modern one. The most frequent medieval Latin designation of the book was simply *Horae* ‘hours’, abbreviated from *Horae beate Marie virginis* ‘Hours of the Blessed Virgin Mary’. In Middle English the book was usually referred to as ‘primer’/‘primmer’.

came to adore him. She presented him in the temple forty days after his birth, where Simeon recognised him as the saviour of mankind and made prophecies regarding his future greatness, and the suffering in store for both Jesus and Mary. Mary's husband Joseph fled with the young mother and the baby Jesus to Egypt, to escape the persecution of King Herod, and returned with them to Nazareth after a period of years. When Jesus was twelve years old, Joseph and Mary lost him in Jerusalem, and he was found in discussion with the learned in the temple.

Mary is mentioned briefly during Christ's years of ministry and miracles, for instance on the occasion of his first public miracle performed at the marriage at Cana, when he turned water into wine, and she is prominent once more, in St John the Evangelist's gospel only, during the events of the Passion at Eastertide, when she stood with St John at the foot of the Cross on which Christ was crucified. In the Acts of the Apostles, who were the first followers of Christ to believe his message and teach it after his death, the narrative is continued from the point where the gospel story ends. In Acts it is said that Mary awaited with the apostles the descent of the Holy Spirit at Pentecost, or Whitsuntide, which took place seven weeks after the Passion, and ten days after Christ ascended to heaven.

In the early centuries of the Christian era many stories of the Virgin were told in what are known as apocryphal narratives and gospels, that is to say, books which did not come to be included in the Bible. These stories fill the gaps, as it were, by providing information about Mary's infancy, and about her later life, the end of her life, and her assumption into heaven and coronation there. Apocryphal stories circulated widely in the Middle Ages, and were translated from Latin into the vernacular languages of western Europe, such as medieval French and English.[2] They were read and heard by both lay and religious audiences. According to these narratives Mary was born when her parents Anne and Joachim were already advanced in years, mirroring the birth of John the Baptist to the elderly Zacharias and Elizabeth as described in the first chapter of St Luke's gospel. Descriptions of Mary's infancy include such features as her parents' presentation of her in the temple when she was a small child, her dedication to the lord, and her desire to serve the woman destined to be the mother of Christ, ten years or so before she knew that she herself was to be that woman.

The Marian material, both biblical and apocryphal, was woven into rich drama, poetry and narrative, as well as into anthems and hymns,

2 See James 1924; Stace 1998.

Offices and Masses. A full account of her life, drawing on biblical and apocryphal sources, is given in the *Ave et gaude* salutations of the Carew-Poyntz Hours (text **10.2**).

In the late tenth and the eleventh century there was a period of monastic reform in England, during which time the Benedictine order was revitalised and strengthened. At this time the Christian order of monks and nuns founded by St Benedict, in the fifth century, was still by far the largest and most important monastic order in Europe. From the late tenth century comes the earliest mention of an Office of Mary, that is to say, a monastic religious service worshipping God, the deity, but expressing also special veneration of Mary. The Office prayers praise her and appeal to her for intercession, asking her to pray to Christ for the salvation of mankind in general, and for the supplicant in particular. There was a text for a regular Saturday Office of Mary from the mid-eleventh century, Saturday being a day set aside for devotion of Mary except when another major festival fell on that day.[3] A full Office of the Virgin was used on Marian feast-days, which celebrated the major events of her life. The feast of her Conception was celebrated on 8 December. This came to be termed the Immaculate Conception, because it was held that Anne conceived Mary without the sin of concupiscence, or sexual desire – the 'original sin' transmitted to posterity by Adam and Eve because of their fall from grace in the garden of Eden.[4]

Mary's Nativity was celebrated on 8 September. Her Presentation in the temple as a small child was remembered on 21 November. The feast of the Annunciation (coinciding with the Conception of Christ) fell on 25 March, and was not the occasion of a major festival in spite of its importance to salvation history. It usually occurred in Lent, shortly before Easter, and the church did not celebrate major festivals other than those of the Passion of Christ at this season. A 'women's festival' was the Visitation, 2 July; on this occasion the pregnant Mary visited her cousin Elizabeth, mother-to-be of John the Baptist. The Nativity of Christ, at Christmas, was celebrated as a festival of Christ, not of his mother. The Purification, when Mary went to the temple for the 'churching' ceremony in which she was cleansed of impurities forty days after giving birth, coincided with the Presentation of Jesus in the

3 See Clayton 1990, 270; 271; Roper 1993, 50. Mary was venerated especially on Saturdays because it was held that after Christ's death on Good Friday she alone remained strong throughout the Saturday in her belief in the Resurrection of Christ, which took place on Easter Sunday. See **10.2** 36.

4 The doctrine of the Immaculate Conception was widely accepted from the late Middle Ages, yet there were some important theologians who rejected it. It was not accepted as a dogma of the Roman Catholic church until 1854.

temple, and with the popular pre-Christian feast of Candlemas, on 2 February.[5] Mary's Assumption into heaven following her death, or 'dormition' (falling asleep), was celebrated on 15 August. Of these events, only the Annunciation, Visitation and Purification are recounted in the Bible. The remaining feast-days are based on apocryphal narratives.

The full Marian Office for all these occasions was recited or sung in monasteries from the tenth or eleventh centuries by those in religious orders, and subsequently also by secular priests in cathedrals, colleges or churches. There was also a simplified version, with fewer variations, known as the Little Office or Hours of the Blessed Virgin Mary. The Little Office remained part of the breviary used in monasteries and secular churches, but it could also be written out separately, especially in manuscripts destined for lay use.[6] Devout lay people tried to emulate the religious life by integrating as much as possible of the Little Office into their daily lives. Once the Office became detached from the breviary, other Offices, psalms and prayers accumulated around it, resulting in the course of time in what we now know as the book of hours.

The production of devotional manuscripts for lay people, such as the book of hours and, before it, the psalter, was encouraged by the church in response to a decree issued by the Lateran Council of 1215. This decree required parish clergy to attend more assiduously than had previously been the case to the spiritual needs of lay parishioners. Friars of the mendicant religious orders, Franciscans and Dominicans, played an important part, alongside secular priests, in the move to produce edifiying texts for the laity. Spiritual guidance of lay people was part of the mission of priests and friars. The earliest book of hours to have survived from medieval England, the mid-thirteenth century De Brailes Hours, shows Dominican influence.[7] The fourteenth-century De Mohun Hours, probably a marriage gift for a young lady from the county of Somerset, has among its supplementary contents a long penitential mendicant poem, probably Franciscan, in Anglo-Norman French (Boston Public Library MS 124, fols 58r–63; Dean and Boulton 2000, no. 789).[8] In the fifteenth century, Dominican influence is still in evidence, for instance in the Bolton Hours (York Minster Additional

5 The occasion continued to be referred to most frequently as 'Candlemas'.

6 See Wieck 2001, 492: 'the Hours had consoled the ordained for hundreds of years before becoming the center of lay devotion in the mid-thirteenth century'.

7 See Donovan 1991, 125.

8 For the original patron of this manuscript see Michael 1982.

MS 2).[9] Another order charged with responsibility for the spiritual guidance of the laity was that of the Austin canons; the Neville of Hornby Hours (British Library MS Egerton 2781) shows their influence, as well as that of the friars.[10]

The Lateran decree included a requirement for thorough preparation of the laity for confession and penance, and there is a strong penitential element in many books of hours. In the fifteenth century, two books that were probably made for a merchant-class individual and family respectively, Isabel Ruddok's Hours (Bristol Public Library MS 14) and the Bolton Hours (York Minster Additional MS 2), contain Forms of confession which take the reader through all the sins that may have been committed (text **25**).

Since the Middle Ages are sometimes regarded as an era of unshaken faith in the tenets of Christian belief, it is of some interest to note that the Form of confession (text **25**) includes a section in which the penitent confesses failure to believe steadfastly in each article of the faith in turn: the Trinity, the conception of Christ by the unblemished Virgin Mary, the incarnation of Christ as God and man, the Passion, the Resurrection, the Ascension, and the Day of Judgement. For the devout, faith was something to be worked at day in and day out, amidst all the vicissitudes of life, with the help of the book of hours.

*

The core text of the book of hours, the Little Office, has psalms, hymns and prayers for each of the so-called canonical hours: matins, lauds, prime, terce, sext, none, vespers, compline. Matins, the 'morning hour', was said or sung in the very early hours of the morning, after midnight and before dawn. It was immediately followed by lauds, and these two first hours are sometimes counted as one, which means that the total number of canonical hours may be given either as eight or as seven. Prime, the 'first hour', was said or sung at dawn, or around 6 a.m.; terce, the 'third hour', at around nine a.m.; sext, the 'sixth hour', at around midday; none, the 'ninth hour', at around 3 p.m.; vespers, the 'evening hour', at around 6 p.m.; and compline, the 'completing hour', just before retiring for the night.[11] In every Office, matins and vespers

9 See Cullum and Goldberg 2000, 21.

10 See Smith 2003, 137–38; 193–94; 256.

11 For a differentiated account of the timing of the hours see Cheney 1997, 9: 'Early medieval custom divided the day into two periods, running from sunset to sunrise and from sunrise to sunset. Within each period were twelve hours, the length of which necessarily varied with the season. The hour which formed 1/12 of the winter night, for example, would be longer than a similar fraction of the summer night. As a consequence of this, the

were the most substantial of the hours, sometimes, indeed, the only ones recorded; in addition to psalms, hymns and prayers, which occur at each hour, matins included extensive readings from scripture, patristics – texts written by the Fathers of the Church – saints' lives, and homilies, or sermons.

The Little Office occurred initially with seasonal variations. There was one form for Advent, the four weeks leading up to Christmas, another for the period from Christmas to the feast of the Purification, or Candlemas (2 February), and a third for the period from Candlemas to Advent. Sometimes there were further subdivisions within Advent and the Christmas period. For lay people the form of the Office used from Candlemas to Advent was generalised, unvaried throughout the year.[12]

As has already been mentioned, the Blessed Virgin Mary is very prominent in the book of hours. When, as could often happen, the book of hours was the most important or the only book that a lay person or family possessed, their devotions were therefore likely to focus very largely on Mary. No doubt the strong focus on Mary was in tune with many people's devotional proclivities, since the cult of Mary flourished in the later Middle Ages, yet this emphasis may have come about, at least in part, by chance. The Little Office originated in an extension of the daily Office recited or sung in honour of God in religious houses rather than as a substitute for it. Only when it became separated from the breviary for convenience of lay use, and other Marian texts accrued around it, did lay worship come to be weighted so heavily towards Mary. From the start, artist-designers of books of hours were at pains to provide accompanying images drawn from Christ's infancy and Passion, and the interweaving of passages from the Office of the Cross with the Little Office also did much to restore the balance.[13]

In the fifteenth century any imbalance was further redressed, whether consciously or not, by the addition of prayers to Jesus. The most powerful and most frequently found of the new supplementary prayers was the sequence of the Fifteen Oes attributed to St Bridget of Sweden (text **9.1**). In the Bolton Hours comes a prayer to Jesus, *Ave Jhesu Christe verbum patris*, with an introductory rubric which ascribes to Christ himself measures to enhance worship of himself as compared with veneration of Mary:

seven "canonical hours," or the times appointed for the services of the Church, similarly varied with the season, until the introduction of hours "of the clock".'

12 This means that if a book of hours prescribes seasonal variations in the Little Office it was probably compiled for use in a religious house. Such is the case, for instance, with the Aldgate Abbey Hours (Reigate, St Mary's Parish Church, Cranston Library 2322).

13 There is an example of such interweaving in text **1**.

> There was a certain clerk in Burgundy who greeted the Blessed Virgin Mary every day with the words 'Hail Mary'. One day Christ appeared to him saying 'You greet my mother every day and are her friend and if you will greet me you will be my friend'. To whom the clerk said, 'Lord, if I knew how to, I would do it gladly'. Then the Lord gave him these words of salutation:
> 'Hail Jesus Christ, word of the father . . .'
> (York Minster Additional MS 2, fols 176r–177r)

*

Most books of hours opened with a calendar recording church festivals and saints' days throughout the year, and included further, in addition to the Little Office,[14] the Office of the Dead, with commendations of the souls of the deceased; set groups of psalms, in particular the Penitential Psalms and the Gradual Psalms (most of which also occur either in the Little Office or in the Office of the Dead); a litany, and further commemorations of the saints.[15]

Both calendar and litany could be 'personalised' to include saints of local and personal interest, and the calendar could be used to record dates significant to owners and their families in addition to religious festivals and feast-days. The additional personal family items in the Tanfield-Neville Hours calendar are exceptionally informative; they give not only the date of Neville family births, marriages and deaths, but also the time of day or night, the phase of the moon and the relevant 'dominical letter' (text **4**). It is thought that Richard III (reigned 1483–85) wrote in his own hand the entry for 2 October in the calendar of an early-fifteenth-century book of hours which came into his possession: *hac die natus erat Ricardus Rex Anglie tertius Apud Foderingay*

[14] Since the Little Office of the Blessed Virgin Mary is the core text of the book of hours, a book of hours without the Little Office is a rarity; usually such an omission would occur only when part of a manuscript has been lost. However, there is at least one exceptional situation, namely in some of the manuscripts made for Bridgettine nuns of Syon Abbey, for instance, the Syon Abbey Hours, and British Library, Cotton Appx 14 (the latter not represented in the present volume). For their daily Office, the nuns of this order, which was founded by St Bridget of Sweden in the fourteenth century, did not use the monastic breviary followed by other orders, and by the monks of their own order. Rather, they had, and still preserve, their own distinctive Office, with readings revealed to the visionary St Bridget. The Bridgettine Office is permeated with Marian readings and prayers, and indeed the order was established in honour of the Virgin Mary. It seems likely that the existence of their own Marian Office led to the omission of the Little Office from their beautiful books of hours.

[15] The commemorations of the saints are usually found within the Little Office, at the end of lauds, in English books of hours; whereas in continental books they tend to be a separate item (see Donovan 1991, 60).

*Anno domini m.ccccliiº* 'on this day was born Richard III king of England at Fotheringay AD 1452'.[16]

The calendar could also include references to dates and seasons noted from pagan antiquity as requiring special measures of caution, such as *dies caniculares* or 'dog days', usually the hottest days of the year, which were considered dangerous to health, and *dies Aegyptici* or 'Egyptian days'. The 'dog days' could last for a month or more each summer, whereas two 'Egyptian days' needed to be calculated for each month. Instructions for this calculation are often given in cryptic Latin verse at the head of a month: one needs to work forwards from the beginning of the month to find the first perilous day, and backwards from the end to find the second. The term *dies Aegyptici* attests medieval European respect for what was seen as a useful ancient Egyptian aid in calculating perilous times.[17]

The Office of the Dead was used at the point of transition from earthly life to death, and to commemorate all the faithful dead, especially one's own friends and relations recently deceased. Furthermore, recited daily, or at least on a frequent and regular basis, it served to remind users of the book of hours of their own mortality and urge them towards a manner of conducting themselves in this life that would lead them safely through all perils to eternal life beyond death. Wieck has pointed out that the Office of the Dead can be read, like numerous supplementary prayers in the book of hours, as protection against sudden death and attendant perils to the soul.[18]

The book of hours contained several psalms within each Hour of each Office, and further set sequences of psalms (from which the Office psalms were frequently drawn, so that a given psalm might occur several times in a manuscript). That the psalms formed the basis of all Offices is not always apparent at first glance when one looks at medieval manuscripts. They were so well known that they were often indicated simply by their incipits, or opening phrases. Whereas a medieval reader was apparently able to work from incipits, modern readers need

16 There has been some discussion as to whether this famous book (Lambeth Palace Library MS 474) might have been compiled originally for female use. Sutton & Visser-Fuchs (1990, 38; 44) consider original female ownership unlikely on the grounds of seasonal variations, male forms in prayers, and supplementary devotions to SS Christopher and George. The seasonal variations, however, would not be surprising if the book was intended for use in a nunnery (see p. 156). Moreover, male forms in prayers are common in books intended for women owners; prayers were sometimes adapted for female use, and sometimes left in the 'unmarked' masculine form. Devotions to St Christopher occur frequently in women's books (see texts **17.9.1–4**).

17 See Harthan 1977, 36.

18 Wieck 1988, 30.

numbers in order to identify and find the psalms, and also need to have the texts written out in full (see text **1** for the psalms used at vespers and compline).

Two different systems of numbering are now in use, which can be confusing. Broadly speaking, one system follows the numbering of psalms in the Vulgate version of the Bible, a Latin translation dating from the fourth century of the Christian era and attributed to St Jerome, which was widely used during the Middle Ages. The other system is that adopted by the Anglican Church from the time of the King James Bible (1611). The present volume follows the Vulgate numbering, and text, because the book of hours belongs more to the Vulgate than to the post-medieval Anglican tradition. Equivalent psalm numbers from the King James Bible are given in brackets.

In the so-called Penitential Psalms, frequently drawn on for the Office of the Dead, the penitent sinner confesses and laments his sins, yet trusts in the lord to hear his prayer and supplications. These psalms usually number seven:

6 (6) *Domine, ne in furore* O Lord, rebuke me not in thy indignation, nor chastise me in thy wrath
31 (32) *Beati quorum* Blessed are they whose iniquities are forgiven, and whose sins are covered
37 (38) *Domine, ne in furore* Rebuke me not, O Lord, in thy indignation; nor chastise me in thy wrath
50 (51) *Miserere mei* Have mercy upon me, O God, according to thy great mercy
101 (102) *Domine, exaudi* Hear, O Lord, my prayer: and let my cry come to thee
129 (130) *De profundis* Out of the depths I have cried to thee, O Lord
142 (143) *Domine, exaudi* Hear, O Lord, my prayer: give ear to my supplication in thy truth: hear me in thy justice

The Gradual Psalms, frequently drawn on for the Little Office, were said to have been recited on the steps (Lat. *gradus*) of the temple in Jerusalem. The apocryphal legend had it that when Mary, aged three, was dedicated by her parents to God, on the occasion of her presentation in the temple she ascended the fifteen steps unaided, and recited on each step one of the fifteen 'psalms of the steps'.[19] The fifteen Gradual Psalms, though at times penitential, express confident faith and trust in God. They are:

[19] Her ascent forms the subject of one of the salutations of Mary in the Carew-Poyntz Hours: 'Hail and rejoice, virgin Mary; offered by your parents to the temple of the lord, you ascended the steps quickly with no-one to guide you; [a feat] beyond the strength of one of your age' (**10.2**, 4).

119 (120) *Ad dominum cum tribularer* In my trouble I cried to the Lord: and he heard me
120 (121) *Levavi oculos meos* I have lifted up my eyes to the mountains, from whence help shall come to me
121 (122) *Letatus sum in hiis* I rejoiced at the things that were said to me: We shall go into the house of the Lord
122 (123) *Ad te levavi oculos* To thee have I lifted up my eyes: who dwellest in heaven
123 (124) *Nisi quia Dominus* If it had not been that the Lord was with us, let Israel now say
124 (125) *Qui confidunt* They that trust in the Lord shall be as mount Sion: he shall not be moved for ever that dwelleth in Jerusalem
125 (126) *In convertendo* When the Lord brought back the captivity of Sion, we became like men comforted
126 (127) *Nisi Dominus aedificaverit* Unless the Lord build the house, they labour in vain that build it
127 (128) *Beati omnes, qui timent* Blessed are all they that fear the Lord: that walk in his ways
128 (129) *Saepe expugnaverunt me* Often have they fought against me from my youth, let Israel now say
129 (130) *De profundis* Out of the depths I have cried to thee, O Lord
130 (131) *Domine non est exaltatum* Lord, my heart is not exalted: nor are my eyes lofty
131 (132) *Memento, Domine, David* O Lord, remember David: and all his meekness
132 (133) *Ecce quam bonum* Behold how good and how pleasant it is for brethren to dwell together in unity
133 (134) *Ecce nunc benedicite* Behold now bless ye the Lord: all ye servants of the Lord: Who stand in the house of the Lord, in the courts of the house of our God

The Gradual Psalms include some penitential verses, and Psalm 129 (130), *De profundis*, 'Out of the depths I have cried to thee, O Lord,' occurs in both the gradual and the penitential sequences. Nonetheless, even the more sombre incipits of Psalms 128 (129) and 129 (130) lead to affirmations of trust and hope. The enemies who have fought the psalmist from his youth could not prevail over him (Psalm 128 (129), 2). The cry from the depths gives way to hope in the Lord: 'Because with the Lord there is mercy: and with him plentiful redemption. And he shall redeem Israel from all his iniquities' (Psalm 129 (130), 7–8).

Several of the Gradual Psalms look for peace. The psalmist has been peaceable with those that hated peace (Psalm 119 (120), 6); he exhorts his listeners to prayer for the peace of Jerusalem, and to let peace be in their strength (Psalm 121 (122), 6–7). The Lord has enabled our soul to escape the enemy 'as a sparrow out of the snare of the fowlers' (Psalm 123 (124), 7). One of the shortest psalms (Psalm 132 (133), see text **5**) extols unity between brothers, and the blessing of eternal life that is unity's consequence. It is safe to assume that for medieval as for modern women, even more than for men, the desire for peace 'within their gates' will frequently have been uppermost in their minds.

The Gradual Psalms resound with promises made to the chosen people, to be understood in the context of the book of hours as the Christian church, and such undertakings are likely to appeal strongly to devout women, particularly through the promises made regarding the fruit of their womb:

> The Lord hath sworn truth to David, and he will not make it void: of the fruit of thy womb I will set upon thy throne. If thy children will keep my covenant, and these my testimonies which I shall teach them: Their children also for evermore shall sit upon thy throne
> (Psalm 131 (132), 11–12)

For women there will also have been particular resonance in the comparison of the wife to the fruitful vine:

> Behold the inheritance of the Lord are children: the reward, the fruit of the womb.
> As arrows in the hand of the mighty, so the children of them that have been shaken.
> Blessed is the man that hath filled the desire with them: he shall not be confounded when he shall speak to his enemies at the gate
> (Psalm 126 (127), 4b–6)
> Thy wife as a fruitful vine, on the sides of thy house.
> Thy children as olive plants, round about thy table
> (Psalm 127 (128), 3–4)

Psalm 127 (128) culminates in a combination of the themes of peace and the blessings of children: 'And mayst thou see thy children's children, peace upon Israel' (Psalm 127 (128), 7). The image of the soul as weaned child can be read as an affirmation of the rightness of women and children's roles, despite the focus on the moment of separation: 'As a child that is weaned is towards his mother, so reward in my soul' (Psalm 130 (131), 4).

In the litany of the saints, invocations of the saints are preceded and followed by prayers to God. In a penitential section the devout petitioner asks to be delivered from sundry evils and perils. Many of the petitions have remained largely unchanged in the Catholic litany over the centuries, though there are additions or deletions from time to time. Some of the saints invoked vary according to locality, or according to the preference of a religious order, community or individual. The litany is often followed by the collect for peace.

*

In addition to the standard contents, many books of hours contained additional prayers and devotions, especially books made during the fourteenth century.[20] Some of the supplementary contents were drawn directly from the liturgy, as was the Little Office, and provided more of the same kind of material. The most remarkable book of hours in terms of additional Marian Offices is the De Vere Hours (Cambridge, Christ's College MS 8);[21] it has further Offices for the Conception, the Nativity, the Annunciation, the Purification and the Assumption of Mary. Very common in later books of hours are two additional prayers to Mary, *Obsecro te* and *O intemerata*,[22] and the sequence of prayers to Jesus, the Fifteen Oes, attributed to St Bridget of Sweden (**9.1**).

Among the most frequent types of supplementary text are prayers to Jesus and Mary for help at the hour of death (**7** and **14**) and indulgenced prayers to Jesus and Mary (**9**). Such prayers reiterate the petitions for salvation of the sinner made in the Little Office, the Office of the Dead and the litany, and in the collects or prayers following psalms. The indulgences guarantee remission of time to be spent in purgatory after death.

Verse or prose salutations to Mary, in Latin and in the vernacular languages, Anglo-Norman French and English, occur frequently. The simplest and most important salutation, learnt by heart and recited by all medieval Christians, is the *Ave Maria*, 'Hail Mary', based on the greeting of the angel Gabriel at the Annunciation, 'Hail . . . the Lord is with thee' (Luke 1, 28) followed by the words spoken by Elizabeth at the Visitation, 'Blessed art thou among women and blessed is the fruit of thy womb (Luke 1, 42). It could be recited alone, often many times over. Inasmuch as this formed a recurrent part of the Little Office, the saluta-

20 See Morgan 1993, 35: 'Very few books of hours in the period could be described as standard in either textual or visual content, and it is in their additional prayers and devotions, many of which are Marian, that the uniqueness of each book is often revealed.'

21 This book was made for Alice de Saunford, who died in 1312; it is not represented in the texts translated here.

22 For modern English translations of these prayers see Wieck 1988, 163–64.

tion belongs to the standard contents of the book of hours. Yet it was also elaborated and incorporated into many other sequences of prayers (for instance, text **3**) which form part of the supplementary contents. In more complex compositions biblical and apocryphal material could be expanded into lengthy salutations. A long Anglo-Norman sequence was added to the De Brailes Hours shortly after the book was made (**10.1**), and a Latin one was included in the original design of the Carew-Poyntz Hours (**10.2**) and the Neville of Hornby Hours, with very fine accompanying illustrations in both manuscripts. These are learned rather than popular compositions, as is the short Bridgettine salutation (**10.3**).

Contemplation of the Joys of Mary is the springboard for numerous further compositions (**12**). The acrostic prayers and the so-called Little Psalter of Our Lady build contemplation of the Joys of Mary into a sequence of psalms, prayers, verses and responses in the manner of a liturgical Office (texts **3** and **11**). Contemplation of Mary's Sorrows is less frequent, although her Compassion was an essential component of medieval Christian worship.[23] Yet prayers by the Sorrows are found in the De Reydon Hours (**13**), and, most exceptionally, the Neville of Hornby Hours has the complete text of a lengthy *Complaint of Our Lady*.[24]

Second only to Mary among female saints venerated in the book of hours was her mother, St Anne. She was celebrated in her own Office and numerous prayers were devoted to her (see texts **16.1–4**). Her cult was strengthened in England at the time of the marriage of Richard II to Anne of Bohemia, in 1383. A feast of St Anne was established, and an Office and a Mass were inserted into service books for the new feast.[25]

In celebration of St Anne an anthem was used that is drawn from Proverbs, the Old Testament book that follows the Psalms:

> *Mulierem fortem quis inveniet? procul & de ultimis finibus pretium eius.*
> *Confidit in ea cor viri sui & spoliis non indigebit . . .*
> Who shall find a valiant woman? Far and from the uttermost coasts is the price of her.
> The heart of her husband trusteth in her: and he shall have no need of spoils.
> (Proverbs 31, 10–11)

23 Richard Pfaff has noted that the Feast of the Compassion of the Virgin did not really become firmly established in England, although a supplementary Mass of the Compassion was included in the Sarum Missal from the late fifteenth century; Pfaff 1970, 97–103.

24 Dean and Boulton 2000, no. 957.

25 See Pfaff 1970, 2; 4.

In the Percy Hours there is an Office of St Anne (text **16.1**) in which the *capitulum*, or chapter reading, for the canonical hour of prime is drawn from the same chapter in Proverbs as the anthem.[26] The text compares the valiant woman to the merchant's ship that brings bread from afar (Proverbs 31, 14); and describes her as one who has considered a field and bought it, and has planted a vineyard with the fruit of her hands (31, 16); who has girded her loins with strength, and has strengthened her arm (31, 17); who does not need to fear for her house in the cold of snow, for all her servants are clothed with double garments (31, 21); she has opened her mouth to wisdom, and the law of clemency is on her tongue (31, 26); her children have risen up and called her blessed, and her husband has praised her (31, 28).

No doubt many users of books of hours were thoroughly familiar with this final chapter of Proverbs, since the description of the Good Wife figured in marriage ceremonies from an early date. Women will have drawn inspiration and strength from it in their relationships with spouse and children, and in their daily interactions with commerce, acquisition of property, cultivating the land, managing a household, and giving counsel.

Further women saints frequently invoked in the book of hours are the New Testament penitent, Mary Magdalen (**17.1–17.4**), and the virgin martyr saints, especially Katherine and Margaret. Whereas the Virgin Mary, ever virtuous and humble, was the lodestar of all, St Mary Magdalen was a great source of hope to penitent sinful women. The key features of medieval stories about Mary Magdalen were conflated from gospel narratives of several women called Mary: she was a sinful woman; she repented of her sins and washed Christ's feet with her hair; she was present at the Crucifixion and she was the first to be greeted by the risen Christ (although medieval accounts, notably Bridgettine writings, sometimes had the risen Christ appear first to his mother Mary). There was no doubting the importance of Mary Magdalen's place in Christian history. Appeals to her were highly recommended for penitent women, especially for those who loved too much, and who were given hope that they might win Christ's love. This hope was founded on a story in the gospel of Luke, of which, by popular tradition, Mary Magdalen came to be the 'heroine'; the sinful woman was forgiven, and elevated, for this moment at least, to a status above Christ's apostles (Luke 7, 44–50).

Some saints were considered particularly helpful with regard to

[26] The same chapter of the 'valiant woman' is used in the Office of St Bridget, Syon Abbey Hours, fol. 42r.

specific ailments or pains. St Margaret was the patron saint of women in labour (**17.2**). St Apollonia was thought particularly helpful for toothache (**17.8**). St Zita is an example of a rare but interesting saint sometimes invoked in women's books of hours – a historical figure who actually lived during the late Middle Ages. She was the patron saint of those who served in households, and regarded as especially helpful in finding lost things (**17.6**). St Christopher was the patron saint of travellers, but in the books of hours he is more often invoked in prayers for protection against the plague (**17.9**)

There are several references to a St Susannah, merged with the apocryphal Old Testament heroine of that name (**17.7**). Susannah is invoked as a true and chaste wife, and also as the 'type' of the unjustly accused innocent. Susannah features in the books of hours not only as an innocent person miraculously saved from danger, beside Daniel, the youths in the fiery furnace, Peter on the water, and Paul in chains, but also quite specifically as a woman whose good name was slurred by the unjust accusations of disappointed would-be lechers. Her help is sought in protecting women against slander, malicious gossip and backbiting.

The fear of imputations of unchaste living is evident in several of the books. An extra petition for protection against malicious backbiting is added to one of Alice de Reydon's prayers (**6.3**). In the De Reydon Hours litany there are two appeals to a saint *Castitas* 'Chastity' (fols 91v, 92r) – perhaps erroneously, but nonetheless tellingly. Hawisia DuBois, at the end of her poem by the Five Joys + celestial joy (**12.2**), cites the miraculous deliverance of the unchaste abbess, just before her final petition for herself, a sinful woman. In the story of the unchaste abbess the newborn son of the abbess is whisked away by Mary for safe keeping with a hermit, and the virginity of the abbess is restored, before the arrival of the investigating bishop who tweaks her breasts in vain for evidence of lactation. The child eventually becomes a bishop himself.[27]

The Form of confession (**25**) includes backbiting – slandering or defaming fellow Christians, to bring them from good to ill repute – among the subdivisions of the deadly sin of envy; and lists it again in a rendering of the ten commandments, just before the confession of sins of the flesh. Perhaps Susannah could help to deliver those defamed by their fellow Christians even when there was some truth in the defamation, just as the Virgin Mary could restore the virginity of the unchaste abbess?

27 For some of the numerous visual images of this tale in women's books of hours see p. 18.

Several books of hours include herbal and other remedies among their supplementary texts. Among the fifteenth-century additions to the Solger Hours are the so-called Salernitan verses (**27**), in which specific herbal recommendations are followed by moral precepts on living a life conducive to health of the whole person. Evidence of belief in the importance and efficacy of herbal recipes is provided by the marginal note, apparently made by Charles VI of France when he gave this book to his daughter Katherine de Valois – wife of Henry V of England – hoping that her eyesight would be improved (see **27** headnote). The Beaufort Hours is of great value, among other things, for the intriguing medical recipes added at the end (**28**).

A protective prayer against the plague added to Elizabeth Scrope's Hours is given incantatory reinforcement by repetition of Latin and Greek words (also Hebrew, in another manuscript). Magic power was traditionally attached to repetition of syllables not necessarily understood, the more exotic the better. A Gaelic healing charm has been identified in the Murthly Hours, National Library of Scotland, MS 21000; it was added in the late fourteenth or early fifteenth century to this manuscript originally made in France, which had travelled via England to Scotland.[28] Ronald Black suggests the possibility that the Murthly Hours' Gaelic charm for pain in the foot is to be placed in the afflicted person's shoe.[29] For healing purposes there are also occasional recommendations for the wearing of prayers or charms in a girdle, for instance in pregnancy (addition to Percy Hours, MS Harley 1260, fol. 230r).

However, more important to the owners of books of hours than slips of paper in the shoe or in the girdle, herbal remedies or charms, was the healing power attributed to prayer. The benefits of prayer for clear wits and physical well-being are attested in the concluding section of the long rubric introducing the Fifteen Oes (**9.1**; see also the headnote to the prayer invoking the Sorrows of Mary (**13**)). It was thought that healing could be achieved by means of prayer, and the observation of moral precepts.

Penance was a sacrament, a religious ritual practice, comprising

[28] See Higgitt 2000, with translations from the Gaelic and commentary by R. Black, who also suggests that the quotation of the two opening lines of the prayer to the Guardian Angel with feminine form *commissam* added to fol. ii v of the manuscript be understood here 'in the context of charms in general, and of written charms in particular' (Higgitt 2000, 333; 343).

[29] Higgitt 2000, 343. Black also describes the likely use of the book of hours as a physical object in healing procedures, perhaps even doused in water; and points out that it could be a potential source of income for its owner.

contrition for sins committed, confession at the prescribed times, atonement or 'satisfaction' imposed by the priest and duly performed, followed by absolution. It was essential for the healing and welfare of spirit, mind and body. Penance is a key theme of the Penitential Psalms, the Office of the Dead, and numerous supplementary prayers. It is perforce a vital ingredient of the Middle English Form of confession (**25**).

Even more important than healing in this life was the assurance of eternal life after death. Constant prayer, penance, and drawing down of indulgences granted by popes or bishops were deemed necessary for oneself and for one's relatives, benefactors and friends. The indulgences guaranteed remission of time to be spent in purgatory after death.

Occasionally there is evidence of a rather more frivolous piety. An additional entry in Eleanor Worcester's Hours gives brief salutations to Mary, very suitable to be recited in anxious times, and very effective in gaining remission of years to be spent in purgatory (**9.4**). The rubric explains that the prayer is to be recited daily, but it does not really matter if one cannot quite remember the words; having them written on a scroll and wearing them in one's girdle will also earn some days of release from purgatory. To be on the safe side, the reader is also advised to remember the Joys.

*

Like the supplementary texts, so also the illustrations and decoration of a book of hours could give it a highly individual character. They helped the user to read and understand her texts, and could even provide an integral part of the meaning of a text. Michael Clanchy stresses the importance of thc images in prayer books that 'allowed their users an active and individual role in religion in the privacy of their own homes,' in contrast to the repetition of standard Latin prayers.[30] Undoubtedly the illuminations and decoration encouraged a form of reading that allowed the reader to dwell devoutly on images as well as words, and to internalise both pictures and prayers. The images could also assist memory, and help the reader to find the right place in her book, and to memorise the most important texts. Their beauty could enhance the pleasure of reading and prayer. Sometimes the images included pictures of the original owners or patrons for whom the book was made, so-called 'donor portraits'. This will have enabled the users

30 Clanchy 2004, 113.

to make these books and prayers their own in a highly individual way, seeing pictures of themselves, perhaps at prayer, as they prayed.[31]

Most of the surviving manuscript books of hours were carefully illustrated, at least in the sections containing the standard contents.[32] Frequently they also contained rubrics – headings or captions written in red – preceding or following a text, or accompanying it in the margins. Such rubrics introduced a new text and could explain to the user when or how a particular prayer was to be recited or read, and even what the benefits might be.

Manuscript illustrations could be directly relevant to the texts they accompanied, and help to focus devotion on the meaning of the texts. When miniatures and historiated initials accompanying the Little Office were drawn from the infancy stories of the Virgin or Christ, they could contribute directly to the meaning of such hymns, prayers and readings as dwelt on in these events. Yet by the late fourteenth century more than half the English books of hours had 'mixed' infancy and Passion cycles in their illustrations of the Hours, and in fifteenth-century England the Passion cycles predominated. This, together with the frequent interweaving of the Little Office and Hours of the Cross, meant that at the canonical hours veneration was directed not only towards the Virgin Mary, but also to the Passion. From the earliest books of hours in England, some artist-designers were at pains to present this dual focus.[33]

However, during the fourteenth century some of the most intriguing *bas-de-page* illustrations (drawn along the bottom of the ruled frame or lower margin of a page) and marginal decorations, even of the standard contents, were drawn neither from infancy cycles nor from the Passion. They could be drawn from miracle stories of the saving of sinners by Mary, as in the case of the unchaste abbess (see p. 15 above) in the Madresfield, Taymouth and Carew-Poyntz Hours.[34] The juxtaposition

[31] Some donor portraits are considered in the 'Interpretive Essay', pp. 154–155.

[32] See Higgitt 2000, 165: 'By 1500 books of hours were the most widely owned type of manuscript book and, to judge from survivals, most were illuminated.' Full illustration of the supplementary texts in a book of hours is unusual, but there are some notable exceptions: the Carew-Poyntz Hours, the Neville of Hornby Hours and the Norwich Hours were fully illustrated throughout, as part of the original design.

[33] See Donovan 1991, 38 *passim*; and p. 6 above.

[34] See Backhouse 1975, 18. The Madresfield Hours, formerly at Madresfield Court, is now in the Getty Library at Wormsley, Buckinghamshire. Other manuscripts which include illustrations of the tale of the unchaste abbess are the Taymouth Hours (British Library, Yates Thompson MS 13), the Carew-Poyntz Hours (Cambridge, Fitzwilliam Museum, MS 48), the Neville of Hornby Hours (British Library, MS Egerton 2781) and the Hours of Mary de Bohun, wife of Henry IV (Copenhagen, Kongelige Bibl., Thott. 547.4°).

of such images and the core text of the book of hours can be understood most readily in penitential terms: however grave one's sins might be, contrition, confession and atonement could lead to forgiveness with Mary's help. Miraculous salvation of the sinner in such examples provided the most compelling evidence of God's mercy and goodness.

Images accompanying the standard contents could also be drawn from contemporary medieval life, for instance from scenes of ladies out hunting and hawking, as in the Taymouth Hours; or from a popular fabliau, or tale, again in the Taymouth Hours. In this manuscript, possibly made for Joan, daughter of Edward II (see p. 151), the Little Office is accompanied by the picture story of a young girl presented as being unnaturally ungrateful to an old knight. He rescued her when she was carried off by a *wodewose* 'wild creature,' and then he killed a young knight who came upon the scene. Each of the three in turn – the wild creature, the old knight and the young knight – laid claim to her (text **26**).

*Bas-de-page* illustrations and decorative borders could include human, animal or grotesque figures, entwined in all kinds of acrobatic and decorative poses, as in the Norwich Hours. British Library MS Harley 6563 has some particularly well-drawn birds, hares with bows and arrows, and a precursor of the cat playing the fiddle with other animals playing different musical instruments.[35] Books of hours, like romances, were often embellished with animal pictures, and the prominence of animal illustrations may well be an English feature. As Christopher de Hamel has pointed out, fifty of sixty-five surviving bestiaries from the twelfth and early thirteenth centuries were made, with illustrations, in England.[36] It is tempting to speculate that the books decorated with well-developed picture cycles featuring animals may have been made for very youthful patrons.[37]

In addition to illumination, decoration, and rubrication there may on occasion be a further visual component to the prayers in a manuscript. For instance, in the prayer for protection against the plague in the Brotherton Hours (**15.2**), the sign of the Cross occurs prominently in

35 See especially fol. 40r. This intriguing manuscript is not represented in the texts translated here.

36 Talk entitled 'Manuscript Beasts' given to the Cambridge Bibliographical Society, 18 February 2004.

37 Donor portraits in the Neville of Hornby Hours include a child, and the marginal scheme includes humans, animals, hybrids (a mixture of the two), and a fox preaching to fowl; the Alphonso Psalter (British Library Additional MS 24686) is an example of a comparable type of manuscript made for a ten-year-old boy, with marginal mermaids, acrobatic apes, and knights fighting griffins and giants; see Smith 2003, 267 and further references there.

the margin at three appropriate points. The sign of the Cross was in itself believed to have healing and redemptive powers.

It was in the thirteenth and fourteenth centuries that the compilers, designers and owners of books of hours were at their most resourceful and inventive in giving expression to worship and devotion in illuminations as well as texts. Art historians Michael Camille, Lucy Sandler and Roger Wieck, among others, have drawn attention to the waning of inventiveness and diversity in the illustration and decoration of English books of hours from the late fourteenth century.[38]

At the time of the Reformation in the early sixteenth century, and later, perceived idolatry in devotion to the Virgin Mary, especially in illustrations of her miracles, could lead to mutilation of images in medieval manuscripts. Sometimes whole leaves were destroyed at this period if they contained full-page images of Mary; sometimes smaller parts of a leaf were cut out, or the surface was scratched over; or historiated initial letters (large initial capitals containing pictures) were mutilated. They often contained a detailed image, such as a portrait of Mary. In Elizabeth Scrope's Hours (Cambridge University Library MS Dd.6.1), and in numerous other books, references to popes and to Thomas Becket, the twelfth-century archbishop of Canterbury who supported the authority of the church over Henry II, have been crossed out. The Madresfield Hours once had two full-page miniatures of Marian miracles preceding each of the hours of the Little Office. Preceding matins it has lost the left half of what may well have been one of the most objectionable miracle stories to a Protestant eye, the tale of the unchaste abbess (see p. 15 above).

*

The Office of the Dead and the Penitential Psalms are sometimes accompanied by miniatures or historiated initials that show tonsured clerks singing. They document the origins of the core text of the book, the Little Office of the Virgin, in the singing of additional Marian anthems after the Hours of the daily divine Office, especially compline. Singing monks also illustrate quite aptly psalms such as no. 95 (96) *Cantate Domino*, 'Sing ye to the lord a new canticle: sing to the Lord, all the earth'. The book of hours lost much of the musical character its component parts once had, as it came to be used by the laity as well as by monks, nuns and priests, in private as well as in public. Yet in nunnery books some elements of communal worship remain, and some of the texts are still likely to be embellished with musical notation. In

[38] See Camille 1987, 40; Sandler 1986, Vol. 1, pp. 38–40; Wieck 1988, 30.

the fifteenth century there was a flowering of polyphony in Marian anthems, in monastic, secular and collegiate establishments.[39] Traces of this musical richness can be found in some nuns' books.

In the Aldgate Abbey Hours the texts, with their seasonal variations and accessory contents, include noted anthems for Marian and other feast-days (see the illustration from the Office for the profession of a Franciscan nun, **5**, plate 2, p. 56). Several of the nunnery manuscripts in the Fitzwilliam Museum Library in Cambridge have musical notation. Fitzwilliam MS 2–1957, for instance, made for Elizabeth Shelford, abbess of Shaftesbury in the early fifteenth century, has music for parts of the Office of the Dead and Commendation of Souls.

*

Just as the survival of music in the nunnery books is a reminder of the anthems' earlier use in a liturgical setting, so also the prevailing use of Latin in English books of hours recalls the origin of the standard contents in church services and rituals. In England, the standard contents of the book of hours were usually written in Latin right up to the end of the Middle Ages. Of the women's manuscripts examined for this study, there is only one exception: English occurs in part of the Little Office in Bodleian Library MS Liturg. 104. Rubrics, headings, prayers of private devotion and other supplementary items could be in Latin or in the vernacular – Anglo-Norman French, English, or most exceptionally Gaelic – or in a combination of these languages. Vernacular rubrics are far more common than vernacular texts; their instructions and explanations in the spoken language helped the reader to understand a Latin text, and use it appropriately.

Inasmuch as the vernacular languages were used, Anglo-Norman French was the more frequently used vernacular language up to the late fourteenth or early fifteenth century; then it gradually ceded to English. The most active trilingual combination of Latin and the vernacular languages is found in the fourteenth century, as for instance in the De Mohun Hours (Boston Public Library MS 124), and the DuBois Hours (New York, Pierpont Morgan Library MS M.700). Further manuscripts in which Latin in the standard contents is supplemented by both Anglo-Norman French and Middle English in rubrics and supplementary contents are the Taymouth Hours (British Library MS Yates Thompson 13) and the Percy Hours (British Library MS Harley 1260). The tendency in such cases is for the Anglo-Norman items to be part of

39 See Roper 1993, 175.

the original compilation, and for the English texts to be later additions. Yet Latin held its own, even in supplementary material.

The large-scale retention, or even reintroduction, of Latin in English books of hours is in contrast to the situation in continental Europe, where there is a steady increase in the vernacular in comparable compilations during the late Middle Ages. The question arises as to what can have caused the continuation, reinforcement or reintroduction of Latin in English manuscripts in the fifteenth century. Several scholars have attributed the delay in the coming of English to the book of hours to the prohibitions on translations of the Bible issued in the Constitutions of Clarendon of 1408.[40] These constitutions, or church laws, were issued by Thomas Arundel (1353–1413), archbishop of Canterbury, in order to counteract Wycliffite texts and teachings in English. John Wycliffe (c. 1329–84) was an English reformer who was active 150 years before the Reformation, and was in some ways a precursor of the later changes of religion that led to the separation between the Roman Catholic Church and the Anglicans. Wycliffe attacked abuses in the church, argued for secular control of the clergy, and appealed to the people in their own language by writing in English and translating the Bible. Since much of the book of hours consists of biblical texts, and the Constitutions of Clarendon prohibited translation of the Bible into the vernacular, it seems reasonable to ascribe the retention of Latin, in part at least, to church censorship and control. Those responsible for the spiritual guidance of the laity will have done everything possible to guard themselves and their flock from the severe punishments imposed by church law, and, after the accession of Henry IV in 1399, by the state. A further reason for the retention of Latin may have been that prayers were felt to be more authoritative and powerful when recited in the learned and venerable language of the church, its scriptures and its priests.

In the few manuscript books of hours with the whole contents translated into English – such as those edited by Maskell[41] and Littlehales[42] – there is some internal evidence to support Wycliffite associations. One of the Middle English manuscripts listed by Maskell, Oxford, Bodleian Library MS Bodley 85, has among its accessory contents a text based on Wycliffe's treatise on the ten commandments. The same Wycliffite text is included in another small Bodleian book of hours in English, MS Douce 246. Douce himself observed further Wycliffite

40 See for instance Erler 1999, 498; 504.

41 A Middle English text was edited from British Library Additional MS 17010 by Maskell 1882, Vol. 3, pp. 1–183 (MS then in Maskell's possession).

42 Littlehales 1895, 1897.

resonances in his manuscript: he noted in it that the Magnificat text corresponds to one in a manuscript belonging either to Wycliffe or to his follower Purvey. A manuscript now in Glasgow, Hunterian Museum MS 512, has the Hours of the Blessed Virgin in Latin and English, following which there are jottings in both languages that include quotations from Wycliffe on the epistle to the Galatians.[43]

The prevalence of Latin in the book of hours leads to the question of lay fluency in the learned language. To what extent could people outside the monasteries read and understand the texts in their books of hours? Could they read enough Latin to pray as instructed? The Hours of Elizabeth the Queen makes provision, entirely in Latin, for one who understands the Latin of the Mass:

> *Si quis latinum intelligat*
> If a person understands Latin and wants to hear the Mass, let her listen to it and to everything the priest devoutly reads out loud, and when he is silent or reads with hushed voice let her read the prayers written out below because they are authorised and taken from the Mass and are full of edification, and when the priest and the listener shall have said the creed, and the priest the absolution, let her read this prayer . . .
> (British Library Additional MS 50001, fol. 147r)

On the other hand, the Carew-Poyntz Hours makes provision, entirely in Anglo-Norman, for one who does not understand the Latin of the Mass:

> *Et si vous n'entendez point le latyn*
> And if you do not understand Latin, say this prayer devoutly when the priest takes in his hands the body of our lord:
> 'Jesus Christ, just as truly as I believe that what the priest takes in his hands in form of bread is your most holy body which suffered death, torment and Passion for all sinners, grant to me a sinner . . .'
> (Cambridge, Fitzwilliam Museum MS 48, fols 27r–v)

Of Margaret Beaufort, mother of Henry VII, we are told that she much regretted not having learnt Latin more assiduously in her youth; but that, such regrets notwithstanding, she could understand enough liturgical Latin to follow the Offices and the Mass.[44] In fact, with regard

43 None of these compilations with contents entirely in English can be shown to have been made for a woman owner.

44 See Mayor 1876, 292.

to the reading of Latin, it is likely that medieval owners of books of hours were in a similar position to medievalists today: some extremely fluent, the majority able to read liturgical Latin with a little prompting, some not able to construe more than a few words.

## List of Texts

## Manuscript Sources of Translated Texts

The entries are structured as follows:

Current location with manuscript reference
Designation in terms of early ownership or current location
Date (often approximate) of original compilation; and of later additions if relevant to text(s) translated
Source of text(s) translated, and of photographic reproductions
Selected references

The manuscripts were made in England unless otherwise stated.

For further information, beyond the few selected references listed here, see especially the institutional resources, which range from hand-written notes by generations of scholars to full online resources. Many libraries have copious trays or folders of information gathered over many years, and also provide online information about their books of hours, sometimes with reproductions of manuscript illuminations: e.g. the British Library in London, the Bodleian Library in Oxford, the Pierpont Morgan Library in New York, and the Walters Gallery in Baltimore (which has 300 Books of Hours, mostly from France and Flanders; not represented in this sample).

Blackburn, Museum and Art Gallery, MS 091.21040
Tanfield-Neville Hours
c. 1440; additions to calendar dating from this time to late sixteenth century
Source of **4**
Refs: Furnivall 1868; Erler 2000

Boston Mass., Boston Public Library MS 124 (formerly MS 1546)
De Mohun Hours
1324–37; fifteenth-century additions from fol. 91
Source of **15.1**
Refs: Bond & Faye 1962, 213; Gee 2002, 148; Haraszti 1955, 72–74; Michael 1982

Bristol City Library; Bristol Public Library MS 14
Isabel Ruddok's Hours
Early fifteenth century; fifteenth-century adddition on fol. 2r

Source of **1**, **17.9.3**, **21**; source of plate 1, p. xii
Ref.: *MMBL* Vol. 2, 209–210

Cambridge, Fitzwilliam Museum MS 48
Carew-Poyntz Hours
1350–60; further additions in late fourteenth century, and fifteenth century
Source of **10.2**
Refs: James 1895, 100–120; Sandler 1986, Vol. 2, no. 130, pp. 143–45

Cambridge University Library MS Dd.4.17
De Reydon Hours
Early 1320s
Source of **6.1**, **6.2**, **6.3**, **7.2**, **8**, **13**, **23.1**, **23.2**
Refs: *CUL Catalogue* Vol. 1, no. 192, pp. 225–26; Gee 2002, 42–44; 138; illustrations 3, 4; Lasko and Morgan 1973, 12–13; Sandler 1986, Vol. 2, no. 67, pp. 75–76

Cambridge University Library MS Dd.6.1
Elizabeth Scrope's Hours
Fifteenth century; late-fifteenth-century additions include Elizabeth Scrope's signature
Source of **22**; source of plate 3, St Anne and the Education of the Virgin, p. 113
Ref.: *CUL Catalogue* Vol. 1, no. 318, pp. 288–89

Cambridge University Library MS Dd.15.19
Agnes Hykeley's Hours
Fifteenth century; fifteenth-century additions at beginning and end, perhaps in Agnes Hykeley's own hand
Source of **9.3**
Ref.: *CUL Catalogue* Vol. 1, no. 873, p. 544

Cambridge University Library MS Ee.6.16
Amesbury Hours; nuns of Fontevrault
Fourteenth century; additions in unlearned hands in items bound up with and preceding calendar and Hours; some extra slips sewn in with additions or modifications
Source of **16.2**, **16.3**, **16.4**
Refs: *CUL Catalogue* Vol. 2, no. 1108, pp. 262–63; Bell 1995, Amesbury 1, p. 103; Kerr 1999

Exeter, Exeter University Library, EUL MS 262
on loan from Syon Abbey; Syon Abbey MS 2
Syon Abbey Hours

Mid fifteenth century; additions later fifteenth century, and sixteenth century
Source of **10.3**, **17.4**, **17.6**
Refs: Bell 1995, Syon 46, pp. 199–200; *MMBL* Vol. 4, 336–342

Leeds, Leeds University Library, Brotherton Collection MS 3
Brotherton Hours
Made in Flanders for the English market
Mid-fifteenth century; supplementary material added in England
Source of **9.2**, **15.2**, **17.2**
Ref.: *MMBL* Vol. 3, 27–30

London, British Library, Additional MS 17012
Fifteenth century; early-sixteenth-century addition at end
Source of **24**
Ref.: BL catalogue for Additional MSS acquired in 1847; Maskell 1882, Vol. 3, 287–88

London, British Library, Additional MS 33385
Beatrice Hours
Thirteenth century; thirteenth-century additions
Source of **20**
Ref.: C. Donovan 1991, esp. pp. 145–46 (regarding excision of illustrations); 190–92

London, British Library, Additional MS 49999
De Brailes Hours
c. 1240
Source of **10.1**
Ref.: Donovan 1991; Morgan 1992–98, Vol. 1, no. 73, pp. 119–121

London, British Library, MS Arundel 318
Arundel Hours
Fifteenth century; late-fifteenth-century additional material
Source of **12.4**
Refs: BL Catalogue of Arundel Manuscripts; Barratt 1992, 279

London, British Library, MS Harley 1251
Eleanor Worcester's Hours
Mid fifteenth century; late-fifteenth-century additions include Eleanor Worcester's book-ownership verse
Source of **9.4**
Refs: BL Catalogue of Harleian Manuscripts; Littlehales 1897, xlv

London, British Library, MS Harley 1260
Percy Hours
c. 1322–1340
Source of **16.1**, **19**
Ref.: BL Catalogue of Harleian Manuscripts

London, British Library, MS Royal 2.A.18
Beaufort Hours
1399–1410; late-fifteenth-century/early-sixteenth century additional items
Source of **17.9.1**, **18.1**, **28**
Ref: Scott 1996, no. 37, Vol. 2, pp. 127–132

London, British Library, MS Sloane 2565
Queen Mary Hours
Early sixteenth century
Source of **17.3**, **17.9.2**
Ref.: BL Catalogue of Sloane Manuscripts

London, British Library, Yates Thompson MS 13
Taymouth Hours
c. 1325
Source of **26**
Refs: Brantley 2002; Brownrigg 1989; Gee 2002, 155; 49–52; 160–61; illustrations 9, 10, 11, 12; Sandler 1986, Vol. 2, no. 98, pp. 107–09

New York, Pierpont Morgan Library MS M.700
DuBois Hours
Fourteenth century; several fourteenth-century additional prayers
Source of **12.1**, **12.2**, **12.3**, **17.7**
Refs: De Ricci 1935–40; Morgan Library Catalogue, http://Corsair.morganlibrary.org; Sandler 1986, Vol. 2, no. 88, pp. 96–98; Smith 2003

Norwich, Norwich Castle Museum MS 158.926/4f.
Norwich Hours
Early-to-mid fourteenth century; almanach calculation for year 1339, fol. 8v
Obit (record of death) of *Katerine Bakon* dated 1377 (*MMBL* reads 1477)
Source of **7.1**, **11**, **14.2**, **17.1**
Refs: Lasko and Morgan 1973, 21–22; *MMBL* Vol. 3, 518; Sandler 1986, Vol. 2, 53–55

Nuremberg, Stadtbibliothek MS Solger 4.4°
Solger Hours
1287–1294
Made in France, for use in France and England
Source of **9.1**, **27**
Ref.: Simmons 1994

Oxford, Bodleian Library MS Gough liturg. 9
Malling Abbey Hours
First half of fifteenth century
Source of **14.1**
Ref.: Erler 2002, 146

Oxford, Bodleian Library MS Liturg. 104
c. 1340
Has arms of Edward III (reigned 1327–1377)
Made for male, passed to female hands
Source of **2**
Ref.: Bodleian Library Summary Catalogue no. 30605

Reigate, St Mary's Parish Church, Cranston Library 2322
Aldgate Abbey Hours
Late fifteenth century
Source of **5**; source of plate 2, p. 56
Refs: Bell 1995, no. 4, p.150; *MMBL* Vol. 4, 201–03

Urbana-Champaign, University of Illinois, Illinois MS 76
Lyte Hours
c. 1390
Made in Flanders for the English market
Source of **3**, **6.4**
Refs: Bradley [c. 1900]; Bond & Faye 1962, 170–71; notes by N.R. Ker in UIUC library, uncat. 016.091, R350 sup.2

York, York Minster Additional MS 2
Bolton Hours
Early fifteenth century
Source of **6.5**, **17.8**, **18.2**, **25**
Refs: Barratt 2005; Cullum and Goldberg 2000; King 1996

## Editorial Conventions

The Modern English translations remain close to the sense of the original Latin, Anglo-Norman or Middle English texts.

They aim to reproduce the line divisions of verse texts, but not their rhyme or syllabification patterns.

Where texts, or more frequently parts of texts, come from the Bible or the breviary, the Douay translation of the Vulgate is followed. The psalms are given with Vulgate numbering (numbering of King James Bible in brackets).

Notes at the head of each text include: the manuscript title, if any, or incipit from the main body of the text (not from the rubric); the manuscript from which the translation is taken; selected references to other manuscripts; the language(s) of any title and introductory rubric, and of the main body of the text; selected bibliographical references; comment on the text.

In the translations, the title and/or incipit, introductory rubrics, any subheadings, and manuscript additions in languages other than the language of the main body of the text, are given in italics. The main body of each text is presented in roman print. This means that the correspondence of language to font varies from one text to another. If, for instance, the main body of a text is in Latin in the original, while the rubrics are in a vernacular, either Anglo-Norman or English, then the translation of the Latin is given in roman, the translation of the vernacular language in italics. Conversely, if the body of a text is in the vernacular, with rubrics and/or supplementary prayer in Latin, then the translation of the vernacular is given in roman, the Latin in italic print. In the case of composite texts in which Anglo-Norman and Latin alternate in the body of the text (as in **8**, **9** and **11**), the translation of the Anglo-Norman is given in roman, the Latin in italic print.

Square brackets [] are used for material added by the translator. This occurs where a title is supplied; or where initial phrases of liturgical texts, usually psalms or prayers, are expanded from abbreviated forms in the manuscript. It occurs where a word is supplied; and very occasionally for explanatory material, e.g. '[kidneys]' explaining the word 'reins' in **1** (but the meanings of more obviously difficult words are given in the glossary); or to supplement geographical information, by supplying the name of the county in which a given place is located, as in 'Mereworth [Kent]' in **4**. Diagonal slash marks \ / are used to enclose material added by a scribe between lines or in margins, or scribal corrections or alterations to a text in the original manuscript.

A longer prayer, hymn or psalm is expanded the first time it occurs; thereafter the opening words are given, with a cross-reference to the previously expanded form.

Footnotes are kept to a minimum. They are used to indicate breaks in a text, as in **2**, and significant alterations or additions made in a manuscript, such as the alteration of feminine to masculine forms in **25**.

Explanatory notes of some words and phrases, and proper names from biblical and later religious history, are given in the glossary.

# The Texts

## 1 Vespers and compline from the Little Office or Hours of the Blessed Virgin Mary with added Commemorations from the Hours of the Cross

*Deus in adiutorium meum intende*

Isabel Ruddok's Hours

Bristol Public Library MS 14, fols 41r–45v

Latin prose and verse

Refs: for the expansion of psalms, *Roman Breviary*; for the expansion of prayers shared with the Mass, see Bruylants 1952, Vol. 2

The Little Office or Hours of the Blessed Virgin Mary can be found with minor variations in most books of hours. Sections from the Hours of the Cross, or the entire Office, are often interwoven with the Little Office, especially in English books of hours. Most of the psalms at vespers and compline of the Little Office are taken from the Gradual Psalms, strongly associated with Mary by the popular tradition that she recited them as she ascended the steps of the temple on the occasion of her Presentation. The exceptions are psalm 12 and psalm 25 at compline. In Isabel Ruddok's Hours, a single commemoration from the Hours of the Cross is added at the end of each Hour of the Little Office. Compline, the last Hour of the day, is often followed by additional prayers, and by the anthem *Salve regina*, as it is here. Following the Little Office and its additional prayers and anthem, on fol. 46, there is written twice, on both sides of the leaf, perhaps in Isabel Ruddok's own hand: *Da michi Issabelle Ruddok famule tue victoriam contra inimicos meos* 'Grant me, your servant Isabel Ruddok, victory over my enemies'. For Isabel's own prayer, see text **21**.

*Here begin Vespers*
God, take heed to help me.
Lord, make haste to help me.
Glory be to the father, [and to the son, and to the Holy Ghost,]
As it was [in the beginning, is now, and ever shall be, world without end].
Alleluia

*Anthem*
After giving birth [you remained an unspotted virgin].

*Psalm [121 (122)]. Letatus sum*
[I rejoiced at the things that were said to me: We shall go into the house of the Lord.
Our feet were standing in thy courts, O Jerusalem.
Jerusalem, which is built as a city, which is compact together.
For thither did the tribes go up, the tribes of the Lord: the testimony of Israel, to praise the name of the Lord.

Because their seats have sat in judgement, seats upon the house of David.
Pray ye for the things that are for the peace of Jerusalem: and abundance for them that love thee.
Let peace be in thy strength: and abundance in thy towers.
For the sake of my brethren and of my neighbours, I spoke peace of thee.
Because of the house of the Lord our God, I have sought good things for thee.
I rejoiced at the things that were said to me].

*Psalm [122 (123)]. Ad te levavi*
To thee have I lifted up [my eyes, who dwellest in heaven.
Behold as the eyes of servants, are on the hands of their masters,
As the eyes of the hand-maid are on the hands of her mistress: so are our eyes unto the Lord our God, until he have mercy on us.
Have mercy on us, O Lord, have mercy on us: for we are greatly filled with contempt.
For our soul is greatly filled: we are a reproach to the rich, and contempt to the proud].

*Psalm [123 (124)]. Nisi quia dominus*
If it had not been that the Lord [was with us, let Israel now say: If it had not been that the Lord was with us,
When men rose up against us, perhaps they had swallowed us up alive.
When their fury was enkindled against us, perhaps the waters had swallowed us up.
Our soul hath passed through a torrent: perhaps our soul had passed through a water insupportable.
Blessed be the Lord, who hath not given us to be a prey to their teeth.
Our soul hath been delivered as a sparrow out of the snare of the fowlers.
The snare is broken, and we are delivered.
Our help is in the name of the Lord, who made heaven and earth].

*Psalm [124 (125)]. Qui confidunt*
They that trust [in the Lord shall be as mount Sion: he shall not be moved for ever that dwelleth in Jerusalem.
Mountains are round about it: so the Lord is round about his people from henceforth now and for ever.
For the Lord will not leave the rod of sinners upon the lot of the just: that the just may not stretch forth their hands to iniquity.
Do good, O Lord, to those that are good, and to the upright of heart.
But such as turn aside into bonds, the Lord shall lead out with the workers of iniquity: peace upon Israel].

*Psalm [125 (126)]. In convertendo dominus*
When the lord brought back [the captivity of Sion, we became like men comforted.
Then was our mouth filled with gladness; and our tongue with joy.
Then shall they say among the Gentiles: The Lord hath done great things for us: we are become joyful.
Turn again our captivity, O Lord, as a stream in the south.
They that sow in tears shall reap in joy.
Going they went and wept, casting their seeds.
But coming they shall come with joyfulness, carrying their sheaves].

*Verse* [repeating the words of the anthem sung before the psalms]
After giving birth you remained an unspotted virgin.
*Response*
Mother of God [pray for us].

*Chapter. Beata es*
Blessed are you, Virgin Mary, who have born the lord; you have conceived the creator of the world who made you; you remain eternally a virgin. Thanks be to God.

*Hymn. Ave maris stella*
Hail star of the sea, holy mother of God, ever-virgin, blessed gate of heaven.
Receiving that word 'Hail' from Gabriel's mouth, ground us in peace, reversing the name of Eve.
Loosen the bonds of the guilty, bring forth light for the blind: cast aside our evils, intercede for all that is good.
Show yourself a mother. May Christ who deigned to be born your son accept our prayer through you.
Maid excelling in meekness, free us from the bonds of sin and make us courteous and chaste.
Grant us a pure life, prepare a safe path for us, so that we may see God and rejoice for evermore.
Praise be to God the father, worship to Christ on high, and to the Holy Ghost; one worship to all three.
Let it be

*Verse*
Grace is in the words of your lips;
*Response*
Therefore God has blessed you without end. Holy Mary, help us.

*Canticle. Magnificat anima mea*
My soul doth magnify the Lord:
And my spirit hath rejoiced in God my Saviour.
Because he hath regarded the humility of his handmaid; for behold from henceforth all generations shall call me blessed.

Because he that is mighty hath done great things to me, and holy is his name.
And his mercy is from generation unto generation, to them that fear him.
He hath shewed might in his arm: he hath scattered the proud in the conceit of their heart.
He hath put down the mighty from their seat and hath exalted the humble.
He hath filled the hungry with good things: and the rich he hath sent empty away.
He hath received Israel his servant, being mindful of his mercy.
As he spoke to our fathers: to Abraham and to his seed for ever.
Glory be [to the father, and to the son and to the Holy Ghost], as it was [in the beginning, is now, and shall be for evermore. Amen]

*Prayer*
Holy Mary, succour the wretched; help the faint-hearted; comfort those who weep; pray for the people; intervene for the clergy; intercede for devout womankind.
Show us [your grace].
Grant us [your servants, almighty God, that we may rejoice in perpetual wellbeing of mind and body: and that through the intercession of the glorious blessed ever-Virgin Mary we may be delivered from present sorrow, and enjoy eternal happiness. Through Christ our Lord]

*Prayer*
Let us bless [the Lord]

*De passione ad vesperas*
[Commemoration] of the Passion at Vespers

*Anthem. De cruce deponitur*
He was taken down from the Cross at the hour of evensong; his strength was hidden in the mind of the godhead. The healer of life underwent this death; alas, the crown of glory now laid low.

*Verse*
We worship you, Lord Jesus Christ, son [of God];
*Response*
Convert us, God of our salvation,
And avert your anger from us.

*[Here begins Compline]*
God, take heed to help me.
Lord, make haste to help me.
Glory [be to the father and to the son, and to the Holy Ghost,
As it was in the beginning, is now and ever shall be world without end].

*Anthem. Cum jocunditate*
With gladness let us celebrate the memory of blessed Mary so that she may intercede for us to our Lord Jesus Christ.

*Psalm [12 (13)]. Usquequo domine*
How long, O Lord, [wilt thou forget me unto the end? how long dost thou turn away thy face from me?
How long shall I take counsels in my soul, sorrow in my heart all the day?
How long shall my enemy be exalted over me? Consider, and hear me, O Lord my God.
Enlighten my eyes that I never sleep in death: lest at any time my enemy say: I have prevailed against him.
They that trouble me will rejoice when I am moved: but I have trusted in thy mercy.
My heart shall rejoice in thy salvation: I will sing to the Lord, who giveth me good things: yea I will sing to the name of the Lord most high].

*Psalm [25 (26)]. Judica me*
Judge me, [O Lord, for I have walked in my innocence: and I have put my trust in the Lord, and shall not be weakened.
Prove me, O Lord, and try me; burn my reins [kidneys] and my heart.
For thy mercy is before my eyes; and I am well pleased with thy truth.
I have not sat with the council of vanity: neither will I go in with the doers of unjust things.
I have hated the assembly of the malignant; and with the wicked I will not sit.
I will wash my hands among the innocent: and will compass thy altar, O Lord.
That I may hear the voice of thy praise: and tell of all thy wondrous works.
I have loved, O Lord, the beauty of thy house; and the place where thy glory dwelleth.
Take not away my soul, O God, with the wicked: nor my life with bloody men:
In whose hands are iniquities: their right hand is filled with gifts.
But as for me, I have walked in my innocence: redeem me, and have mercy on me.
My foot hath stood in the direct way: in the churches I will bless thee, O Lord].

*Psalm [128 (129)]. Sepe expugnaverunt*
Often have they fought [against me from my youth, let Israel now say.
Often have they fought against me from my youth: but they could not prevail over me.

The wicked have wrought upon my back: they have lengthened their iniquity.
The Lord who is just will cut the necks of sinners: let them all be confounded and turned back that hate Sion.
Let them be as grass upon the tops of houses: which withereth before it be plucked up:
Wherewith the mower filleth not his hand; nor he that gathereth sheaves his bosom.
And they that pass by have not said: The blessing of the Lord be upon you: we have blessed you in the name of the Lord].

*Psalm [130 (131)]. Domine non est exaltatum*
Lord, my heart is not exalted: [nor are my eyes lofty.
Neither have I walked in great matters nor in wonderful things above me.
If I was not humbly minded, but exalted my soul:
As a child that is weaned is towards his mother, so reward in my soul.
Let Israel hope in the Lord, from henceforth now and for ever].

*Anthem. Cum jocunditate* [repeating the anthem that precedes the psalms]
With gladness let us celebrate the memory of blessed Mary so that she may intercede for us to our Lord Jesus Christ.

*Chapter. Sicut synamomum*
With the odour of cinnamon and balsam I have spread fragrance, like choice myrrh I have spread a sweet perfume.
Thanks be to God.

*Hymn. Virgo singularis* [repeating the concluding verses of *Ave maris stella* sung at vespers]
Maid excelling in meekness, free us from the bonds of sin and make us courteous and chaste.
Grant us a pure life, prepare a safe path for us, so that we may see God and rejoice for evermore.
Praise be to God the father, worship to Christ on high, and to the Holy Ghost; one worship to all three.

*Verse. Ecce ancilla*
Behold the handmaid of the Lord;
*Response*
Be it unto me according to thy word.

*Anthem. Glorificamus*
We glorify [you, mother of God, because Christ is born of you; save all that glorify you].

*Canticle. Nunc dimittis*
Now thou dost dismiss [thy servant, O Lord, according to thy word in peace.
Because my eyes have seen thy salvation,
Which thou hast prepared before the face of all peoples:
A light to the revelation of the Gentiles, and the glory of thy people Israel].

*Anthem. Glorificamus.*
We glorify you, mother of God, because Christ is born of you; save all that glorify you.
Show us [your grace] and we shall be saved.

*Prayer. Gratiam tuam quaesumus*
Lord, we beseech you, infuse our minds with your grace, so that through the angel's message we may gain knowledge of the incarnation of your son Jesus Christ, and by his Passion and Cross be led to the glory of his Resurrection. By Christ [our Lord, who lives and reigns with you in the unity of the Holy Spirit, God, world without end]
Let us bless the Lord.
Thanks be to God

*Hora completorii datur sepulture*
Commemoration of the Burial at compline

At the hour of compline the noble body of Christ, hope of life to come, is given over to burial. He is anointed with spices, the scriptures are fulfilled. May this death be for me a constant memory of anguish. To you, Christ, I put it with humble logic: you who suffer for my sake, with the fire of love, be my solace in death and anguish.

*Verse*
We worship you, Christ, and bless you.

*[Post-compline] Salutation of Holy Mary*

*Anthem. Salve regina*
Hail queen, [mother of mercy; hail life, our sweetness and our hope.
To you we cry, outlawed sons of Eve,
To you we sigh with lamentation and weeping in this valley of tears.
Come quickly therefore, you our advocate,
Turn your merciful eyes upon us, and after this exile show us Jesus, the blessed fruit of your womb].

*Verse*
Hail Mary full of grace, [the Lord is with you];
*Response*
Blessed are you [among women and blessed is the fruit of your womb, Jesus].

*Prayer. Omnipotens sempiterne deus*
Almighty everlasting God, who through the workings of the Holy Ghost miraculously prepared the body and spirit of the glorious virgin and mother, Mary, to be a worthy dwelling-place for yourself; grant that through the pious intercession of her, to whom we address our commemoration and litany, we may be delivered from evils in the present world, and from perpetual death.
Amen

## 2 Vernacular verses from the Hours of the Cross

*Swete Jhesu Cryst goodis sone of lyve*
Oxford, Bodleian Library, MS Liturg. 104, fols 48r–88r
Middle English verse
Ref.: *IMEV* 3230 (this manuscript not listed)
Ed.: Brown 1924, no. 34, pp. 50–51, from this manuscript

The Hours of the Cross in Bodleian Library, MS Liturg. 104, is unusual in two ways: firstly, it contains Middle English verse renderings of the final Latin prayer for each Hour (translated here); secondly, it is written out as an independent Office as far as terce, fols 48r–64v, and then, after at least one missing leaf, continues from sext interwoven with the Hours of the Little Office, fols 65r–88r. At vespers and compline they correspond in subject matter, though not in wording, to the material translated from the Latin Hours of the Cross in **1**. For the blind soldier referred to at none see **8** headnote, and glossary under 'Longinus'.

[*Matins*]
Sweet Jesus Christ, living son of God,
May your Passion, your Cross, your death, your five wounds
So palliate our sinful souls in your judgement,
Now and at the hour of death, that we are not destroyed.
Deign to give power and grace to those who are to live,
And for their repose forgive their sins.
To holy church and our kingdom grant love and peace,
And to us, sinful wretches, life without end;
You, who live as king, God and man without end,
Father, son and Holy Ghost, bring us to that bliss.

[*Prime*]
At the first hour Jesus was brought before Pilate,
Many false testimonies were given against him,
His shins were beaten, his hands were bound,
They spat in his face, they saw nothing of heaven.

[*Terce*]
At dawn the Jews clamoured for the Cross,
In scorn he was clothed in a purple pall,
On his shoulder he carried the Cross to the place of suffering
[. . .][1]

[*Sext*]
At midday Jesus Christ was nailed to the Cross,
Between two thieves he hung for our sake,
For thirst of harsh pain he was given gall to drink;
The holy Lord so fair of form redeemed all our sins.

[*None*]
At the ninth hour Lord Christ departed from this life,
He cried 'Eloi', sent his holy spirit to his father.
A soldier with a sharp spear pierced his side,
The earth quaked, the sun shining all around turned dark.

[*Vespers*]
At evensong he who paid dearly for us was taken down;
His might, his strength, bowed low in deep sorrow;
This death he sustained, healer of all woe;
Alas, there they laid low the crown of worship.

[*Compline*]
He was assigned to burial at the last hour,
Christ's noble body, hope of life to come.
He was anointed with spices to fulfil holy writ.
May I always remember in sorrow his death.

## 3 Acrostic psalms and anthems

*Oraciones de sancta Maria incipiunt que intitulantur secundum litteras huius diccionis* ***MARIA***

Lyte Hours

Urbana-Champaign, University of Illinois MS 76, fols 156v–159r

Latin prose and verse

Refs: Bradley [c. 1900]; for the anthems see Meersseman 1958–60; for the acrostic device worked into the pattern of the *Corona Beatae Mariae Virginis* attributed to the thirteenth-century Franciscan St Bonaventure, see Reichl 1973, 97–98; for the Latin prayer occurring also in the Hours of Richard III see Sutton and Visser-Fuchs 1990, 57–58 (Lyte Hours copy not noted)

1 There is a leaf missing at this point.

Acrostic devotions in which the opening letters of prayers or psalms spell out a divine name are not uncommon. The private devotions of the medieval rule for anchoresses, the *Ancrene Wisse*, also include an acrostic sequence of five Marian prayers interspersed with canticle and psalms, in which the Gradual Psalms are drawn upon, as in this sequence from the Lyte Hours. Great importance was attached to the number five, as represented in the Five Wounds of Christ and, as here, in the Five Joys of Mary: Conception, Nativity, Resurrection, Ascension, Coronation of Mary in heaven. The Latin prayers to God invoking the Joys occur also in the Little Psalter of Our Lady, **11**. The last one, *Deus qui beatam virginem Mariam super choros angelorum exaltasti*, is found also in the Hours of Richard III.

The structure of the devotions in the Lyte Hours is as follows: 5 x Latin psalm/canticle + anthem + verse (+ response) + prayer. The opening letters of both psalms and anthems spell the name **MARIA**. In the psalms: Magnificat for **M**; gradual psalm 119 (120) for **A**; psalm 118 (119), 17 for **R**; gradual psalm 125 (126) for **I**; gradual psalm 122 (123) for **A**. In the anthems: ***M**ater ora filium*, ***A**ve regina celorum*, ***R**egina celi letare*, ***I**mperatrix infernorum*, ***A**ve stella matutina*.

*Prayers of St Mary ordered according to the letters of this word **MARIA***

1 *Canticle. **M**agnificat*
[see text **1**, at vespers]

*Anthem. **M**ater ora filium*
Mother, pray to your son
That after this exile
He will give us joy
Without end.

*Verse*
Hail Mary, [the Lord is with you. Blessed are you among women, and blessed is the fruit of your womb].

*Prayer. Deus qui respiciens humilitatem ancille tue*
God, who seeing the humility of your handmaiden made fertile her virginal womb through the Holy Spirit, and filled her soul with ineffable joy, grant us that we may obtain by prayer the grace of true humility in this present life; and that through this we may become co-regents with your virgin mother, through Christ our Lord.

2 *Psalm 119 (120). **A**d dominum cum tribularer*
In my trouble I cried [to the Lord: and he heard me.
O Lord, deliver my soul from wicked lips, and a deceitful tongue.
What shall be given to thee, or what shall be added to thee, to a deceitful tongue?
The sharp arrows of the mighty, with coals that lay waste.

Woe is me, that my sojourning is prolonged: I have dwelt with the inhabitants of Cedar: my soul hath been long a sojourner.
With them that hated peace I was peaceable: when I spoke to them they fought against me without cause].

*Anthem. Ave regina celorum*
Hail queen of heaven,
Mother of the king of angels;
O Mary, flower of virgins,
Like rose or lily,
Pray to your son
For the salvation of the faithful.

*Verse*
Hail Mary

*Prayer. Deus qui sine materno dolore in lucem prodiens*
God, who coming into the light without maternal suffering preserved the seals of chastity intact, and irradiated your mother with double joy, grant us purity of mind and body so that following you we may see the unspotted lamb, pure in heart with the virgin in the heavenly home. Through Christ our Lord

3 *Psalm [118 (119), from verse 17].* ***R****etribue servo tuo*
Give bountifully to thy servant, [enliven me: and I shall keep thy words:
Open thou my eyes: and I will consider the wondrous things of thy law.
I am a sojourner upon earth: hide not thy commandments from me.
My soul hath coveted to long for thy justifications, at all times.
Thou hast rebuked the proud: they are cursed who decline from thy commandments.
Remove from me reproach and contempt: because I have sought after thy testimonies.
For princes sat and spoke against me: but thy servant was employed in thy justifications.
For thy testimonies are my meditation: and thy justifications my counsel.
My soul hath cleaved to the pavement: quicken thou me according to thy word.
I have declared my ways, and thou hast heard me: teach me thy justifications.
Make me to understand the way of thy justifications: and I shall be exercised in thy wondrous works.
My soul hath slumbered through heaviness: strengthen thou me in thy words.

Remove from me the way of iniquity: and out of thy law have mercy on me.
I have chosen the way of truth: thy judgments I have not forgotten.
I have stuck to thy testimonies, O Lord: put me not to shame.
I have run the way of thy commandments, when thou didst enlarge my heart].

*Anthem.* ***R**egina celi letare*
Queen of heaven rejoice;
Alleluia, for the one you were worthy to bear,
Alleluia, has risen as he foretold;
Alleluia, pray to God for us,
Alleluia

*Verse*
Hail Mary

*Prayer. Deus qui in cruce moriens matris dolorem*
God, who dying on the Cross beheld the sorrow of your mother with the eyes of compassion,
And turned the severity of this numbing blow to joy through your Resurrection,
Make us one day participants in your resurgence
And co-inheritors of virginal glory.
Through Christ [our Lord]

4 *Psalm [125 (126)].* ***I**n convertendo*
[See text **1**, at vespers]

*Anthem.* ***I**mperatrix infernorum*
Empress of hell below,
Lady of the heavens above,
Gateway of heaven, hope of the guilty,
Wellspring of mercy, support of the wretched,
Mediator for sinners, mother of God, praise of the saints
And vessel of holiness,
Those who are lying in the depths raise up from wickedness
And be a gracious mother to the impure;
Give means of life to your servants at the moment of death,
A light to those straying in blindness; be the right path,
Intercede to your son that for our vices
The severe judgement of God shall not consign us to torment,
ut after the death of the flesh lead us to heaven
Where peace is, and glory. Amen

*Verse*
Hail Mary, the Lord is with you;

*Response*
Blessed [are you among women, and blessed is the fruit of your womb, Jesus].

*Prayer. Deus qui gaudium matris tue te ascendente*
God, who augmented the joy of your mother when you ascended to heaven
And showed the way for sinners to get there,
Make us desire you perfectly in this life,
And lift the eyes of our mind constantly to you, our God.
Through Christ [our Lord]

5 *Psalm [122 (123)]. Ad te levavi oculos meos*
[see text **1**, at vespers]

*Anthem. Ave stella matutina*
Hail morning star,
Healer of sinners,
Salvation of the world and queen,
Virgin alone worthy to be invoked against the arrows of the enemy;
Set firm your shield of salvation, the title of your miraculous power.
You are the root of Jesse in which God made
Aaron's rod bear almond blossom,
To take away the shame of the world.
You are the sheepskin on which rain fell,
Imbued with celestial dew,
Yet still with dry fleece. In this prison
Shine on us graciously, full of the grace of God;
O chosen bride of God, be to us the right way
To eternal joy, where there is peace and glory,
And hear us always with pious ear, gentle virgin Mary.

*Verse*
Hail Mary [the Lord is with you; blessed are you among women];
*Response*
Blessed [is the fruit of your womb, Jesus].

*Prayer. Deus qui beatam virginem Mariam super choros*
God, who exalted the blessed virgin Mary above the choirs of angels
And crowned her as queen at your right hand above all other creatures,
Grant us a place in your glory, and let us behold you ever with your virgin mother.
Through our Lord Jesus Christ your son, who lives and reigns with you in the unity of the Holy Spirit, world without end.

## 4 A calendar: family records

*The byrth of Margaret Nevill*

Tanfield-Neville Hours

Blackburn Museum and Art Gallery MS 091.21040, fols 1–6 (in blank spaces of Calendar) + last fly-leaf

Most of the entries are in Latin. The following are in English: heading in lower margin of September leaf, announcing birth of Margaret Neville; introductory phrase 'This first day of May' for the record of her first marriage, to Robert Southwell; record of her second marriage, to William Plumbe; record of re-marriage of Margaret Neville's husband William Plumbe on last fly-leaf

Refs: Cheney 1997; Erler 2000; Furnivall 1868

The entries record significant dates for the entire life span of Margaret Neville (1520–75), and just beyond: her birth, her marriage, the births of her five children, the deaths of her parents, the death of her first husband, her re-marriage, her death, and lastly the re-marriage of her second husband. The text gives the date of birth of Margaret Neville's first son as 24 March 1536, which appears to a modern reader to pre-date her marriage by five weeks. However, by medieval reckoning in England this was the last day of the year 1536, since the new year began on 25 March. The translation gives the date according to modern reckoning: 24 March 1537. The system of dating official documents by the regnal year has been common practice from ancient up to modern times, and 'was copied by popes, bishops, kings, dukes, and lesser men' (Cheney p. 3). Presumably the copying of this practice by 'lesser men' or women, such as the Neville family members, or chaplains or clerks in their service, lent additional weight to such calendar entries. The dominical letter is given for the deaths of the mother and the first husband of Margaret Neville, and for the birth of each of her five children. 'There are seven possible relationships of the days of the week to the calendar of the year, and the letters A to G were used to indicate the cycle of seven days beginning at 1 January. The dominical letter for the year is the letter allocated, according to this system, to the first Sunday in the year' (Cheney, p. 8). The dominical letter was essential for the learned calculation of the date of Easter undertaken by the church. For the calendar of family events, however, it may have something of the quality of popular astrological prognostication, like the information frequently given regarding the state of the moon.

1 [*26 September 1520*]

*The birth of Margaret Neville, daughter of Sir Thomas Neville, knight*

Note that Margaret Neville, daughter of Thomas Neville, knight, and Lady Katherine Fitzhugh, his wife, was born at Mereworth [Kent] on the feast of saints Ciprian and Justina, that is to say on

Wednesday the twenty-sixth day of September, in the year of our lord 1520, around the twelfth hour. The moon was full. Her godfather was the abbot of Boxley, and truly her godmothers were the abbess of Malling, and Lady Wyatt; and I [the abbess of Malling] was present at her baptism.

2 [*Sunday 20 August 1527*]
On this day in the year of our lord 1527 died Lady Katherine Fitzhugh, wife of Lord George Fitzhugh and daughter of Lord Dacre of Gilles Land, latterly spouse of Thomas Neville, knight, member of the council of King Henry VIII. The dominical letter was F. May her soul find mercy before the throne on high.

3 [*1 May 1536*]
*This first day of May*, in the year of our lord 1536, and the twenty-eighth regnal year of King Henry VIII, the right worshipful Sir Robert Southwell, knight, and Lady Margaret his wife, daughter and heiress of Sir Thomas Neville, knight, were married at Mereworth.

4 [*24 March 1537*]
Thomas Southwell, firstborn son of Robert Southwell and Margaret his wife, was born at Mereworth around the eleventh hour before noon on the twenty-fourth day of March, in the twenty-eighth regnal year of King Henry VIII, the year of our lord 1537. The moon was full. The dominical letter was G.

5 [*14 December 1538*]
Francis Southwell, second son of Robert Southwell, knight, and Margaret his wife, was born at Holywell in the county of Hertford around the fourth hour a.m. on the fourteenth day of December in the thirtieth regnal year of King Henry VIII, the year of our lord 1538. The dominical letter was F.

6 [*18 March 1540*]
Anna Southwell, eldest daughter of Robert Southwell, knight, and Margaret his wife, was born very early in the morning at Mereworth on the eighteenth day of March in the thirty-second regnal year of King Henry VIII, the year of our lord 1540. The dominical letter was C.

7 [*29 May 1542*]
On this day died Thomas Neville, knight, one of the brothers of George Neville, knight, Lord Abergavenny, in the year of our lord 1542, and the thirty-fourth regnal year of King Henry VIII.

8 [*21 September 1542*]
On the twenty-first day of September, the feast-day of St Maurice and his companions, Dorothea, second daughter of Robert Southwell, knight, and Margaret his wife, was born at Mereworth,

in the thirty-fourth regnal year of King Henry VIII, around the fifth hour p.m., in the year of our lord 1542. The dominical letter was A.

9 [*4 September 1543*]
Henry Southwell, third son of Robert Southwell, knight, and Margaret his wife, was born very early in the morning at Mereworth on the fourth day of September in the thirty-fifth regnal year of King Henry VIII, in the year of our lord 1543. The dominical letter was G.

10 [*26 October 1559*]
Robert Southwell, knight, husband of Lady Margaret Southwell, daughter and heiress of Thomas Neville, knight, died between noon and 1 p.m. on Thursday the twenty-sixth day of October 1559, in the first regnal year of Queen Elizabeth; and he lies buried in the right-hand part of the choir in the parish church of Mereworth in the county of Kent. The dominical letter was A.

11 [*13 November 1561*]
*On Thursday the thirteenth day of November 1561 William Plumbe, gentleman, and Lady Margaret Southwell, widow, were married at Mereworth in Kent.*

12 [*25 December 1575*]
Margaret, sole daughter and heiress of Thomas Neville, knight, widow of Robert Southwell, knight, and wife of William Plumbe, gentleman, died on Sunday the twenty-fifth day of December 1575 at Wyddial in the county of Hertford, aged fifty-five years.

13 [*9 June 1579*]
*On Tuesday in Whitsun week, being the ninth of June 1579, and in the twenty-first regnal year of our most gracious sovereign Queen Elizabeth, William Plumbe and Elizabeth Gresham, widow, were married in the parish church of Fulham.*

## 5 Office for the profession of a Franciscan nun

*Suscepimus deus misericordiam tuam in medio templi tui*

Aldgate Abbey Hours

Reigate, St Mary's Parish Church, Cranston Library 2322, fols 157r–162r

Latin

Refs: Maskell 1882, Vol. 3, 331–359, 'The Order of Consecration of Nuns'; Metz 1954, esp. pp. 211–12; Bruylants 1952, vol. 2, for expansion of prayers drawn from the missal; Yardley 1990, 319–322, for modern transcription of the musical notation of *Amo Christum* and

*Anulo suo* as found in the Consecration of Virgins in Cambridge University Library MS Mm.3

The *Amo Christum* and *Anulo suo* are taken from the liturgy of the virgin martyr St Agnes; both prayers are regularly used in rituals for the consecration of nuns. Hagiography tells that when St Agnes was wooed by a worldly suitor she rejected him, using these verses to declare her love for Christ, and tell the unwelcome wooer that her heavenly bridegroom had already given her the ring of marriage. The imagery of the ring and crown, or bridal wreath, recalls the secular marriage ceremony. Metz draws attention to the dramatic quality of the consecration rituals, and suggests that they play an important part in the development of medieval drama. As is customary in Offices with musical notation, anthems and some psalms are sung to relatively simple chants, while the responsorium, in this case *Amo Christum*, has a complex musical setting. The central declaration of love for Christ is therefore highlighted by the music. See plate 2.

*Office for the profession of a sister*

*Anthem. Suscepimus deus misericordiam tuam in medio templi tui*
Lord, we have received your mercy in the midst of your temple.

*Verse*
Glory be to the father [and to the son and to the Holy Ghost],
*Response*
As it was in the beginning, [is now and ever shall be, world without end].

*Afterwards the psalm shall be sung*
[*Psalm* 132 (133)]. *Ecce quam bonum*
Behold how good [and how pleasant it is for brethren to dwell together in unity:
Like the precious ointment on the head, that ran down upon the beard, the beard of Aaron,
Which ran down to the skirt of his garment: As the dew of Hermon, which descendeth upon mount Sion.
For there the Lord hath commanded blessing, and life for evermore].

[*Verse* ]
Glory be to the father [and to the son and to the Holy Ghost],
[*Response*]
As it was [in the beginning, is now and ever shall be, world without end].

*Then the prayer. Kyrie eleison*
Lord have mercy. Christ have mercy. Lord have mercy.

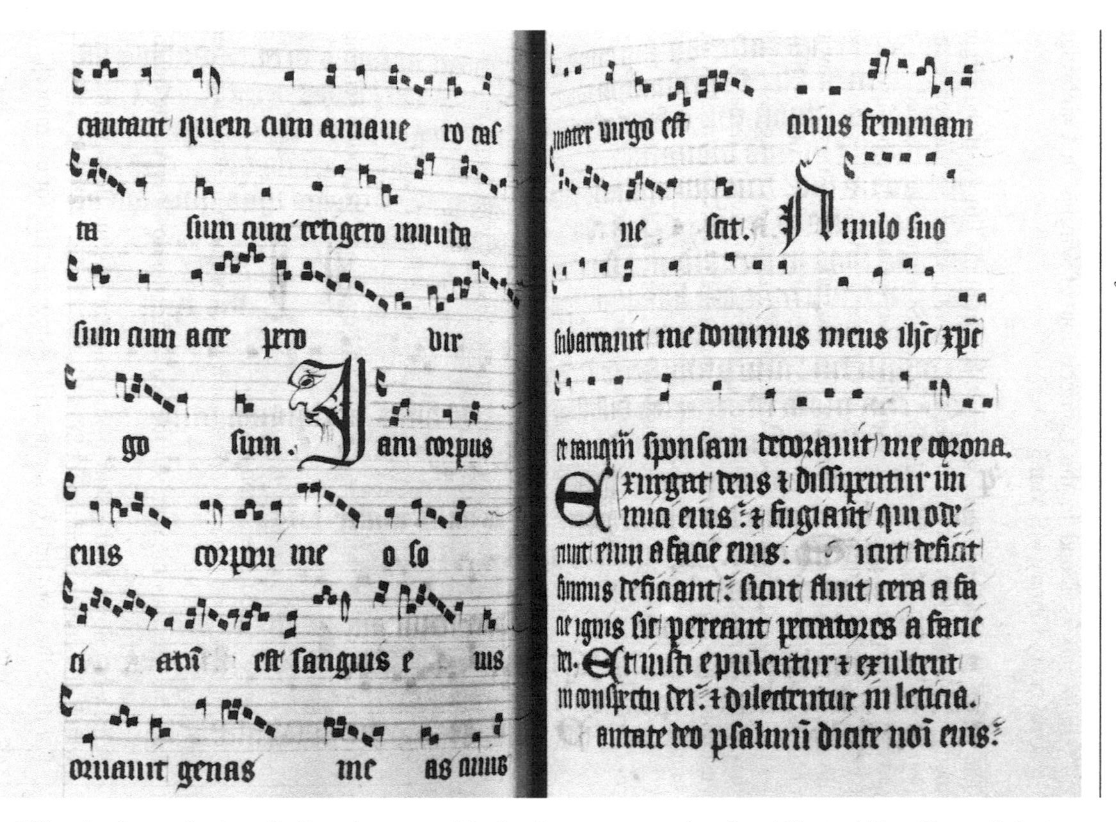

2. Office for the profession of a Franciscan nun. Music of responsory and psalm. Aldgate Abbey Hours, Reigate, Cranston Library 2322, fols 158v–159r, original size of ruled space 13.8 x 8.5 cm, see text **5**

Our father
[*inaudibly as far as*]
Lead us not into temptation
*Response*
But deliver us from evil.

*Verse*
Save your maidservant,
*Response*
My God, whose hope is in you.

*Verse*
Send her, Lord, the help of the Holy Spirit
*Response*
And guard over her in Syon;

*Verse*
Let the enemy make no progress in ensnaring her,
*Response*
Let the son of iniquity have no power to harm her;

*Verse*
Lord, be to her a tower of strength
*Response*
In the face of the enemy.

[*Verse*]
Lord, hear [our prayer]
*Response*
And [let my] cry [come unto you].

*Prayer. Subjectum tibi populum*
[O Lord, may the grace of heaven extend to] your obedient people, [and cause them always to obey your commandments. Through our Lord Jesus Christ]

*Prayer. Acciones nostras quaesumus aspirando preveni*
[O Lord,] we beseech you that our actions may be inspired by grace [and performed with your help; so that each of our prayers and deeds may stem from you, and end as you began it. Through our Lord Jesus Christ]

*Responsory. Amo Christum in cuius thalamum introibo*
I love Christ whose chamber I shall enter;
Whose mother is a virgin; whose father has known no woman;
Whose organ sings to me in sweet modulations;
When I love him I am chaste; when I touch him I am pure;
When I receive him I am chaste.
Already his body is joined to my body;

His blood has adorned my cheeks,
Whose mother is a virgin, whose father knows no woman.

*Anthem. Anulo suo subarravit me dominus Jhesus Christus*
With his ring the Lord Jesus Christ has espoused me and his crown has adorned me as bride.

*Psalm 67 (68). Ex[s]urgat deus & dissipentur inimici eius*
Let God arise, and let his enemies be scattered: [and let them that hate him flee from before his face.
As smoke vanisheth, so let them vanish away: as wax melteth before the fire, so let the wicked perish at the presence of God.
And let the just feast, and rejoice before God: and be delighted with gladness.
Sing ye to God, sing a psalm to his name: make a way for him who ascendeth upon the west: the Lord is his name.
Rejoice ye before him: but the wicked shall be troubled at his presence, who is the father of orphans, and the judge of widows.
God in his holy place: God who maketh men of one manner to dwell in a house:
Who bringeth out them that were bound in strength; in like manner them that provoke, that dwell in sepulchres.
O God, when thou didst go forth in the sight of thy people, when thou didst pass through the desert:
The earth was moved, and the heavens dropped at the presence of the God of Sina, at the presence of the God of Israel.
Thou shalt set aside for thy inheritance a free rain, O God: and it was weakened, but thou hast made it perfect.
In it shall thy animals dwell; in thy sweetness, O God, thou hast provided for the poor.
The Lord shall give the word to them that preach good tidings with great power.
The king of powers is of the beloved, of the beloved; and the beauty of the house shall divide spoils.
If you sleep among the midst of lots; you shall be as the wings of a dove covered with silver, and the hinder parts of her back with the paleness of gold.
When he that is in heaven appointeth kings over her, they shall be whited with snow in Selmon. The mountain of God is a fat mountain.
A curdled mountain, a fat mountain. Why suspect, ye curdled mountains?
A mountain in which God is well pleased to dwell: for there the Lord shall dwell unto the end.
The chariot of God is attended by ten thousands; thousands of them that rejoice: the Lord is among them in Sina, in the holy place.
Thou hast ascended on high, thou hast led captivity captive; thou hast received gifts in men.

Yea for those also that do not believe, the dwelling of the Lord God.
Blessed be the Lord day by day: the God of our salvation will make our journey prosperous to us.
Our God is the God of salvation: and of the Lord, of the Lord are the issues from death.
But God shall break the heads of his enemies: the hairy crown of them that walk on in their sins.
The Lord said: I will turn them from Basan, I will turn them into the depth of the sea;
That thy foot may be dipped in the blood of thy enemies; the tongue of thy dogs be red with the same.
They have seen thy goings, O God, the goings of my God: of my king who is in his sanctuary.
Princes went before joined with singers, in the midst of young damsels playing on timbrels.
In the churches bless ye God the Lord, from the fountains of Israel.
There is Benjamin a youth, in ecstasy of mind.
The princes of Judah are their leaders. The princes of Zabulon, the princes of Nephthali.
Command thy strength, O God: confirm, O God, what thou hast wrought in us.
From thy temple in Jerusalem, kings shall offer presents to thee.
Rebuke the wild beasts of the reeds, the congregation of bulls with the kine of the people; who seek to exclude them who are tried with silver.
Scatter thou the nations that delight in wars: ambassadors shall come out of Egypt: Ethiopia shall soon stretch out her hands to God.
Sing to God, ye kingdoms of the earth: sing ye to the Lord:
Sing ye to God, who mounteth above the heaven of heavens, to the east.
Behold he will give to his voice the voice of power: give ye glory to God for Israel, his magnificence, and his power is in the clouds.
God is wonderful in his saints: the God of Israel is he who will give power and strength to his people. Blessed be God].

*Anthem. Veni sancte spiritus*
Come Holy Spirit, fill the hearts of the faithful
And kindle in them the fire of your love.
Strengthen, God, what you have created in us,
In your temple which is in Jerusalem.
Its foundations are in the sacred hills;
The lord loves the gates of Syon
Beyond all the tabernacles of Jacob.
Glorious things of thee [are spoken]

*Psalm [116 (117)]. Laudate dominum omnes gentes*
O praise the Lord, all ye nations: [praise him, all ye people:

For his mercy is confirmed upon us: and the truth of the Lord remaineth for ever].

[*Verse*]
Glory be to the father, [and to the son and to the Holy Ghost]
[*Response*]
As it was [in the beginning, is now, and ever shall be, world without end].

*Verse. Memento congregacionis tue*
Remember your congregation,
*Response*
Who have been yours since the beginning.

## 6 Prayers at Mass

The Mass culminates in the Eucharistic ritual of consecration of bread and wine, elevation (where the priest lifts up the holy sacrament), and communion, preceded and accompanied by many prayers. The prayers were spoken in Latin by the celebrant, a priest, and while some were spoken out loud and could be followed by all worshippers who had received appropriate instruction, others were spoken sotto voce, in a quiet voice. Lay people were therefore encouraged to read or recite their own prayers during this time; they were also encouraged to include 'levation prayers' in their programme of private devotions at home. Further prayers which focus on the Passion, and therefore on the sacrifice of flesh and blood celebrated in the Eucharist, are the 'Threefold Pity of Jesus', **8**, and the 'Fifteen Oes of St Bridget', **9.1**. These prayers, too, may have been used as prayers at Mass as well as for private devotion.

### 6.1 *[B]eaus sire deu omnipotent*

De Reydon Hours
Cambridge University Library MS Dd.4.17, fol. 76r
Anglo-Norman verse
Manuscripts include Boston Public Library MS 124, fols 109v–110v
Ref.: Dean and Boulton 2000, no. 731 (CUL Dd.4.17 not listed)

All the prayers on fols 75v–78r in the Cambridge manuscript were written on what were perhaps originally blank leaves at the end of a gathering. One leaf has been excised after fol. 78, then a new gathering begins. The hand is similar to that of the main body of this beautifully illuminated and decorated manuscript. However, the writing is smaller, and the initial capitals are often missing; spaces were left for historiated or decorated initials, and never filled.

Noble Lord, almighty God,
Just as I truly believe
That the priest holds here and now
Your flesh as sacrament,
So, truly, Lord,
Amend my wretched life
That I have spent in gluttony,
In wrath, envy and lechery,
In deceit and covetousness,
Contrary to holy church.
Lord, just as I acknowledge truly
That I have sinned vilely,
So let me sin no more,
Nor enter into any embroilment;
Rather let me mend my ways.
Grant me confession before death,
And then let me live
Where I may serve you
With stable heart and pure life,
Through the prayers of St Mary,
And give me strength and power
To pay all that I owe,
And turn my soul towards you.

**6.2** *[S]ire deus ostryez moy qe cele verroye croyz*

De Reydon Hours

Cambridge University Library MS Dd.4.17, fol. 76r

Anglo-Norman prose

No ref. found in Dean and Boulton 2000

See note on additions to the manuscript, **6.1**

Lord God, grant that the true Cross, which was honoured with your holy body and bathed in your holy blood and which touched your holy flesh, be my shield and defence against the devil, so that he may have no power to harm or entrap me.
Lord God, protect me against the malice of all men and women who are hostile to me, so that it may have no power to harm me.

**6.3** *[B]eau sire deus si verrayement cum vus preistes char*

De Reydon Hours

Cambridge University Library MS Dd.4.17, fol. 76r–v

Anglo-Norman prose

Manuscripts include Percy Hours, British Library MS Harley 1260, fol. 165r–v

Ref.: Dean and Boulton 2000, no. 872 (this manuscript not listed)
See note on additions to the manuscript, **6.1**

The link between Susannah and requests for protection against backbiting and slander is here made specific in a scribal addition to the second section of the text. For Susannah's importance in such protection, see also texts **17.7**, **20.1**, **21**.

1 Noble Lord God, just as truly as you took flesh and blood in the virgin Mary and with this flesh suffered death on the Cross in order to save us from the pains of hell, and with this flesh rose again from death to life and with this flesh ascended into heaven and with this flesh will come to judge the dead and the living, just as truly, Lord, as this is true, and I believe it, I pray you to have mercy on me.

2 Gentle Lord Jesus Christ, just as truly as you delivered the three kings from Herod's power and St Susannah from the crime and blame imputed to her, \save me from slander and blame/; and [just as truly as you delivered] Daniel from the lion's pit and St Peter from danger of death, and led your people out of the land of Pharaoh to the promised land, and redeemed us by your precious blood, just as truly I pray you, gentle Lord Jesus Christ, have pity and mercy on me and pardon all the sins I have committed in heart and body, waking and sleeping, and pardon all those who on my account have sinned or are sinning, and pardon all who wish me well, and grant me true confession and true repentance, and time to make amends and lead such a life in this world that before death I may worthily and devoutly receive your precious body, in honour of you and holy church and the salvation of my soul and forgiveness of sins and to the confusion of the enemy, and maintain the peace of holy church and absolve all Christian souls. Amen

3 [Say] five times *Our father* to God, in honour of the five wounds of our Lord; may he guard your body and soul, and protect all you love from all evils.

**6.4** *Jhesu my maker to thy lyknesse that madist me*

Lyte Hours

Urbana-Champaign, University of Illinois MS 76, fols 151v–152v

Middle English prose rubric and text, with Latin insets *Panis quem ego dabo* 'The bread that I shall give' and *Ego sum panis vivens* 'I am the living bread'

*These following prayers shall be said before receiving the blessed sacrament of the altar*

1 Jesus my creator, who made me in your likeness from nothing, more lacking in reason than all other creatures, and after I had sinned you restored me to bliss through your precious Passion; since I am now to receive your blessed body, sacred in form of bread, wash away all my sins with your precious blood, heal and comfort us with your holy sacrament which is ordained to be our medicine and life, through which we shall live with you and dwell with you and you in us, for, Lord Jesus, so you said to your apostles when you ordained: 'The bread that I shall give is my flesh for the life of the world. Whoever consumes me shall live through me.'

2 O Jesus, who through your divine might made this holy sacrament, your precious body, give me grace to receive it with purity of soul, with love, awe and steadfast belief; and, benign Jesus, make me worthy and able to receive your precious body devoutly with all reverence and meekness and heavenly rejoicing in your blessed presence. O blessed, sacred body in form of bread, enter into my soul to fasten it to you in perfect charity, so that I may live according to your will. O heavenly food, O joy of angels, O strength of the soul, truly you said, 'I am the living bread that descended from heaven; whoever will eat of this bread shall live for ever', for, most blessed Jesus, you left your precious body here to be our spiritual strength.

**6.5** *Jhesu my Lord welcom thu be*

Bolton Hours

York Minster Additional MS 2, fols 206r–207r

Rubric with indulgence and text in Middle English rhyming verse; followed by brief Latin prayer to Mary

Ref.: *IMEV* 1734; this MS listed in *IMEV* Suppl.

Ed.: Brown 1939, 181–83

The words *Agnus dei* 'Lamb of God' occur three times during preparation for the Eucharist.

*For every time people say this prayer*
*Between* Lamb of God *and the elevation,*
*They will have in their crown*
*Two thousand years of pardon*

Jesus my Lord, I welcome you,
As I see you here in flesh and blood,
Truly both man and God,
As I know with certainty.
This holy flesh and this blood
You received for our good

From a maiden humble in spirit,
And you laid that flesh on the Cross,
When the blood gushed out from your side,
Out of a wound amazingly great,
In order to save all mankind,
And for us to remember you for ever;
And this you did, as we say,
And rose again on the third day,
And this same flesh with its five wounds
You raised again from death to life,
And then you ascended into heaven,
To make us be with you on high,
And before long you will come
To the terrifying Day of Judgement,
To judge all mankind
According to what they have said or done.
As truly, Lord, as I believe this,
Let me never lose your joy;
By the power of this sacrament,
Lord, let me never more be harmed.
Guard me against sin and shame
In worshipping your holy name,
Protect me against all perils
And give me grace to dwell with you
By virtue of your body here
In the priest's hands on the altar,
And preserve me always with your grace
And grant me a place in heaven.
Jesus Christ, by charity,
Grant, Lord, that it be so,
And show mercy to me always
In worship of the Trinity.

*Hail and rejoice, Mary mother of our Lord Jesus Christ, queen of heaven, mistress of the world, empress of hell; have pity on me and on all Christian people.*

### 7 Prayers to Jesus for help in penance and at the hour of death

Many medieval prayers to Jesus and his mother Mary ask for help at the hour of death. They are traditionally linked with the request to be granted true penance, because of the belief that a person who died 'unprepared', without the sacraments of penance and extreme unction, would go to hell. This gave rise to great fear of sudden death.

**7.1** *Jhesu le fiz Marie ky verays deux verais hom*
Norwich Hours
Norwich Castle Museum MS 158.926.4f., fols 152v–153v
Anglo-Norman prose
Ref.: Dean and Boulton 2000, no. 946

It is possible that the 'sinful woman' petitioner is Katherine Bakon, whose obit is entered in the manuscript for the year 1377. She may well have been the original owner; the prayer could have been written by or for her. See also **17.1** headnote.

Jesus son of Mary, true God and true man, just as truly as you deigned to take flesh of the glorious lady saint Mary who is mother and maid, and then willed this flesh to suffer and bleed on the true holy Cross, to redeem us sinners from death to life, so I truly implore your mercy and beseech you to have mercy on me, a sinful woman, and pardon me the sins I have committed in this world, and grant me true confession before my end and true contrition on the day of my death, and that I may truly atone in this life for my wrongdoings against your will and your commandments; and grant me, Lord, upright faith and firm hope in you on the day of my death, and that I may receive your holy body on the day when my soul departs from this body, which may help me gain salvation so that the devil cannot harm my body or soul, nor in any way gain possession of the body for which you deigned to suffer so glorious a death, and shed your holy blood.

**7.2** *[B]iaus sire deu fiz le pere*
De Reydon Hours
Cambridge University Library MS Dd.4.17, fols 75v–76r
Anglo-Norman rubric and verse prayer
Ref.: Dean and Boulton 2000, no. 891 (this manuscript not listed)
See note on additions to the manuscript, **6.1**

*Whoever says this prayer every day*
*Will never die a bad death in this world*
*Amen*

Noble Lord God, son of the father,
Who commended your sweet mother
To St John the Evangelist,
Who mourned and grieved at your death
As he stood beside the Cross,
Tenderly weeping tears from his eyes
For his great pity, and lamented
The holy death he was beholding,

Lord, for love of him
Grant me this day
To live honourably in this world,
And grant me grace and virtue and vigour
To combat the devil,
And all malignant spirits;
Grant me so to live
That my soul may never perish
Through evil or sin that I may commit,
But rather, through your grace,
At my life's ending
Let me be joined with you
In your blessed company;
You took flesh for us
From Mary virgin and mother;
Through her love and intercession
Accept my request,
You, who live and reign
With God the father, perfect God,
In the unity of the Holy Spirit.
Amen

*Hail Mary, grace is with you*

## 8 The threefold pity of Jesus

[*E*]*n remenbrance de les troys pitez nostre Seignur*
De Reydon Hours
Cambridge University Library MS Dd.4.17, fol. 75v
Anglo-Norman 'remembrances' with Latin prayers and psalms.
No ref. found in Dean and Boulton 2000
See note on additions to the manuscript, **6.1**

'Longinus' is the name given in medieval narratives, and especially drama, to the soldier who pierced Christ's side with a sword. In such narratives Longinus was often portrayed as blind; his blindness was cured by the touch of Christ's blood. See also **2** at none, and **9.1** 15.

*In remembrance of the threefold pity of our Lord*

1 The first was when he saw his mother standing beside the Cross and weeping tears of blood.
*Our father [who art in heaven, hallowed by thy name. Thy kingdom come, thy will be done, on earth as it is in heaven. Give us this day our daily bread. And forgive us our trespasses, as we forgive those*

*that trespass against us. And lead us not into temptation: but deliver us from evil. Amen]*
*Hail Mary*

*Psalm* [12 (13)]. *Usquequo domine*/
*How long, O Lord, wilt thou forget me unto the end?*
[see text **1**, first psalm for compline]

2 The second was when the thief who hung beside him cried for mercy, and he took pity and had mercy on him; just as truly may he show pity and mercy to me.
*Our father*
*Hail Mary*

*Psalm [25 (26)]. Judica me*
[see text **1**, second psalm for compline]

3 The third was when Longinus pierced his side with a lance and cried to him for mercy, and he showed mercy and took pity on him; just as truly may he grant pity and mercy to me and to all my friends alive and dead.
*Our father*
*Hail Mary*

*Psalm* [85 (86)]. *Inclina domine aurem*
*[Incline thy ear, O Lord, and hear me: for I am needy and poor.*
*Preserve my soul, for I am holy: save thy servant, O my God, that trusteth in thee.*
*Have mercy on me, O Lord, for I have cried to thee all the day.*
*Give joy to the soul of thy servant, for to thee, O Lord, I have lifted up my soul.*
*For thou, O Lord, art sweet and mild: and plenteous in mercy to all that call upon thee.*
*Give ear, O Lord, to my prayer: and attend to the voice of my petition.*
*I have called upon thee in the day of my trouble: because thou hast heard me.*
*There is none among the gods like unto thee, O Lord: and there is none according to thy works.*
*All the nations thou hast made shall come and adore before thee, O Lord: and they shall glorify thy name.*
*For thou art great and dost wonderful things: thou art God alone.*
*Conduct me, O Lord, in thy way, and I will walk in thy truth: let my heart rejoice that it may fear thy name.*
*I will praise thee, O Lord my God, with my whole heart, and I will glorify thy name for ever:*

*For thy mercy is great towards me: and thou hast delivered my soul out of the lower hell.*
*O God, the wicked are risen up against me, and the assembly of the mighty have sought my soul: and they have not set thee before their eyes.*
*And thou, O Lord, art a God of compassion, and merciful, patient, and of much mercy, and true.*
*O look upon me, and have mercy on me: give thy command to thy servant, and save the son of thy handmaid.*
*Shew me a token for good: that they who hate me may see, and be confounded, because thou, O Lord, hast helped me and hast comforted me].*

## 9 Indulgenced prayers to Christ and the Blessed Virgin Mary

### 9.1 The Fifteen Oes, attributed to St Bridget of Sweden

*O domine Jhesu Christe eterna dulcedo te amantium*

Solger Hours

Nuremberg Statdbibliothek MS Solger 4.4°; rubric fols 1r–3r; prayers fols 3r–8v

Rubric in English, prayers in Latin

Ref.: for St Bridget of Sweden, see Sahlin 2001

Middle English text, without rubric, ed.: Maskell 1882, Vol. 3, pp. 275–283

These prayers are found in many fifteenth-century books of hours, and in other manuscripts; the rubric with its indulgence was rather frequently defaced or excised at the Reformation. The prayers focus vividly on the Passion. Remembrance of the sacrifice of body and blood is linked with the Eucharist, or Holy Communion, the central sacrament of Christianity held to date from the Last Supper of Christ with his disciples. The Eucharistic link is evident especially in the first prayer, and again in the eighth. It is possible that the prayers were sometimes used at Mass by the laity, like the prayers in **6** above. In addition to the main focus on the Passion, drawn from the New Testament, the prayers draw on the Old Testament for some of the images of Christ: as maker of the world, alpha and omega, king, lion, wellspring, and vine. Towards the end, the prayers turn more towards contemplation of the suppliant's own death, and requests for Christ's help at the moment of death.

*A woman solitary and recluse, desiring to know the number of the wounds of our Lord Jesus Christ, prayed to God that through his special grace he would show her the wounds of his bitter Passion, and at the last our Lord spoke to her and said: 'Say every day for a whole year*

*fifteen* Our fathers *and fifteen* Hail Marys *and at the year's end you will have worshipped every wound in my body and tallied the number of them.' And our Lord said that for every man or woman who says these* Our fathers *and the prayers which follow every day for a whole year, fifteen departed souls from among their kindred shall be delivered from the pains of purgatory, and fifteen meritorious relatives shall be preserved in good life. And whoever says these prayers every day shall have grace and knowledge of perfection and bitter contrition for his sins. And our Lord said further: 'Whoever says these prayers in the prescribed manner, fifteen days before death shall [receive] my holy body, and I shall defend that person from the perils of the sea. Therefore all who can read should say these orisons of my bitter Passion every day for cure of their own ills.'*

*Near to this woman dwelt a holy man to whom she recounted this revelation, and he revealed it to an abbess, and she told it to her sisters and bid them say these orisons. And some said them with great devotion, and some not wanting to trespass did as they were told, and some did so unwillingly, and partly under constraint. And afterwards the same holy man, one day while he was resting, was ravished by a vision in a fair field, and a very delightful well appeared to him, and the well was full of precious stones. By the same well were seen the aforementioned sisters, and some drew from it with great ease, and some with less, and some scarcely gained a drop, and then it was revealed to the holy man that the aforesaid well betokened the three states of the sisters saying their prayers.*

*Then the holy man told this same revelation to the abbess and she told it to her sisters, who were very glad, and the ones who at first said their prayers without great devotion mended their ways and said them with fervent desire.*

*Subsequently, one night this holy man heard a great noise and a hideous cry as if all the forest had been knocked down and torn up by the roots, and he went out of his cell and conjured one of the devils to tell him what the noise was, and the devil answered that there was an old chattering person dwelling in the same wood who said a prayer every day through which the devils suffered great harm, because it was so pleasing and delightful to God that the devils lost many souls through the power of that prayer. And though a man had lain in sin for twenty years, yet if he says these prayers God will forgive him his sins, and defend him against temptation, and keep his wits, and protect him against sudden death. And God says that if a man's soul drinks of his blood he will never thirst, and God will put before him the sign of his bitter Passion to defend him against all enemies. And before his death God will be there with his mother and will lead his soul to everlasting bliss, and will give him a draught of the chalice of his godhead. And if his soul were to suffer pain of purgatory our Lord will change it into pain of this world, and bring his soul to bliss. It is said that this woman's name was St Bridget, queen of Sweden, who received many revelations and the grace of God.*

1 *O domine Jhesu Christe eterna dulcedo te amantium*
O Lord Jesus Christ, eternal sweetness of those who love you, joy exceeding every pleasure and every desire, saviour and lover of sinners, who attested that all your delight was to be with the sons of men, and for man you became man at the end of time; remember all your premeditated plan and the suffering you sustained in your human body at the time of your redeeming Passion in your divine heart, preordained by the eternal heart. Remember the sorrow and bitterness in your mind when at the Last Supper you gave your disciples your body and blood, and washed their feet, consoling them as you foretold your imminent Passion. Remember all the trembling of anguish and affliction which you bore in your delicate body before the Passion on the Cross, when after the threefold prayer and sweating of blood you were betrayed, arrested by the chosen people, accused by false witnesses, unjustly condemned by three judges, innocently condemned in the chosen city at Easter-time in the flower of your bodily youth, stripped of your own clothing and clothed in alien garments, buffeted in your eyes, and your face covered and whipped, tied to a pillar and scourged, crowned with thorns, beaten across the head with a rod, and lacerated with innumerable other insults; I pray you, by the memory of these things that preceded your true Passion on the Cross, grant me contrition, pure confession, due satisfaction and remission of all my sins in this life before my death.
*Our father*
*Hail Mary*

2 *O Jhesu mundi fabricator*
O Jesus maker of the world, whom truly no measurements can encompass to the limits, who hold the earth in your hand, remember the bitter suffering you felt when they first nailed your very gentle hands to the Cross with blunt nails and pierced your most delicate feet, when you submitted to their will to as they inflicted pain upon pain through the wounds, and pulled and stretched you the full length and width of the Cross so cruelly that the joints of your limbs came apart; I beseech you by the memory of that most holy and bitter suffering on the Cross to grant me awe and love of you.
*Our father*
*Hail Mary*

3 *O Jhesu rex celestis*
O Jesus, celestial king and healer, remember the livid languor and suffering you felt, raised up on the high rood of the Cross, in all your torn limbs, none of which remained in its right place, so that no

sorrow could be found like your sorrow, because from the sole of your foot to the crown of your head there was no health in you; and then unmindful of all your suffering you prayed to your father for your enemies, saying 'Father, forgive them, they know not what they do;' through this clemency and the memory of that suffering, grant that the memory of your most bitter Passion give full remission of all my sins.
*Our father*

4 *O Jhesu vera libertas angelorum*
O Jesus, true liberty of angels, paradise of delights, remember the terror and horror you suffered when all your enemies stood about you like the most ferocious lions and maltreated you with buffeting, spitting and tearing with fingernails and other unprecedented tortures; through all these words of scorn, harsh beatings and dire torments, Lord Jesus Christ, and through the sufferings which your enemies inflicted on you, I beseech you to deliver me from all my enemies visible and invisible, and let me beneath the shadow of your wings find the protection of eternal salvation.
Our father

5 *O Jhesu speculum caritatis eterne*
O Jesus, mirror of eternal love, remember the grief you suffered when you beheld in the mirror of your serene majesty the predestined lot of your chosen people, who were to be saved by the merits of your Passion, and the reproof of the evil multitude who were to be damned; and through the bottomless depth of your pity which you then extended to us, lost sinners without hope, and especially which you showed towards the thief on the Cross, saying 'Today you will be with me in paradise,' I beseech you, holy Jesus, to show me your mercy at the hour of my death. Amen
*Our father*

6 *O Jhesu rex amabilis*
O Jesus, loving king, true friend most to be desired, remember the grief you suffered, hanging naked and wretched on the Cross, and all your friends and known adversaries stood there, and you found no comforter but only your beloved mother in bitter sorrow of spirit, most faithful to you, standing there, whom you commended to your beloved disciple saying 'Mother, behold your son;' I beseech you, holy Jesus, by the sword of sorrow that pierced her soul at that moment, to have compassion on me in all my bodily and spiritual tribulations and afflictions, and comfort me in every time of trouble.
*Our father*

7 *O Jhesu fons inhauste pietatis*
O Jesus, fount of mercy ever-flowing, who out of the depth of your love said on the Cross 'I thirst,' that is, you long for the salvation of

the human race; lead our desires, we pray, to every work of perfection, and cool and extinguish entirely in us the thirst for carnal concupiscence and food of worldly love.
*Our father*

8 *O Jhesu dulcedo fons cordium*
O Jesus, sweetness and wellspring of hearts and bountiful honey of souls, through the bitterness of vinegar and gall that you bore for us and tasted at the hour of death, grant us your body and blood, most excellent remedy and consolation of our souls.
[*Our father*]

9 *O Jhesu regalis virtus*
O Jesus, royal power and delight of minds, remember the anguish and sorrow you suffered through the bitterness of death and the insults of the Jews when you cried with a great voice that you were abandoned by God your father, saying 'God, my God, why have you abandoned me?' For this anguish I beg you not to abandon us in the anguish of our death, O Lord our God.
*Our father*

10 *O Jhesu alpha et omega*
O Jesus, alpha and omega, and strength amidst all, remember that from the crown of your head to the sole of your foot you immersed yourself in the water of the Passion for us, in the width and magnitude of your wounds; teach me, who am too much immersed in sin, in true charity your immense message.
*Our father*

11 *O Jhesu abyssus profundissime misericordie*
O Jesus, bottomless well of mercy, I beg you by the great depth of the wounds which penetrated your flesh, the marrow of your bones, and bowels, that you will lift me up, who am immersed in sin, and hide me from your face within the folds of your wounds until your wrath has passed, O Lord.
*Our father*

12 *O Jhesu veritatis speculum*
O Jesus, mirror of truth, token of unity, chain of love, remember the innumerable wounds inflicted on you from the crown of your head to the sole of your foot, and the lacerations of the Jews, and how you were reddened with your most holy blood, how great the suffering you bore in your virgin flesh for us. Holy Jesus, what more could you have done that you did not do? Holy Jesus, I beseech you to inscribe all your wounds in my heart with your precious blood, so that in them I may read your suffering and love and persevere in grateful thanksgiving to the end of my life.
*Our father*

13 *O Jhesu leo fortissime*
O Jesus, mighty lion, immortal and unconquerable king, remember the sorrow you suffered when all the strength of your heart and body entirely failed, and with bowed head you said, 'It is accomplished.' By this suffering and grief, have pity on me at the last ending of my departing spirit, when my soul will be in anguish and my spirit troubled.
*Our father*

14 *O Jhesu unigenite*
O Jesus, only begotten son of the almighty father, radiance and likeness of his substance, remember the humble commendation with which you commended your spirit, saying, 'Father, into your hands I commend my spirit'; and you died for our redemption with lacerated body and pierced heart, with a loud cry and bowels torn open. By this precious death I beseech you, king of saints, give me strength to resist the devil, the world, flesh and blood, so that dead to the world I may live in you; and at the last hour of my going hence, receive my exiled and pilgrim spirit as it returns to you.
*Our father*

15 *O Jhesu vitis vera et fecunda*
O Jesus, true and fruitful vine, remember the plentiful flowing of your blood, which you poured out as if pressed in abundance from clusters of grapes, when you trod the press on the Cross, and offered blood and water for us from the deep wound in your side made by the centurion's lance, so that few or no drops of blood remained in you; and then you were suspended on high like a bundle of wood, and your delicate flesh faded and the moisture of your bowels dried up and the marrow of your bones withered; by this most bitter Passion and most precious pouring out of blood, O gentle Jesus, wound my heart; and may tears of penitence and love be with me day and night, and convert me entirely to you, so that my heart may always be a dwelling-place for you, and my conduct be pleasing and acceptable to you until the end of my life, and sufficient in merit, so that after the end of this life I may deserve to praise you with all your saints for ever and ever. Amen
*Our father*
*Hail Mary*
*The Creed*

## 9.2 Passion prayer

*Domine Jhesu Christe te adoro in cruce pendentem*

Brotherton Hours

Leeds University Library, Brotherton Collection MS 3, fol. 226r

Latin prose text followed by indulgence in English

Ref.: *MMBL*, Vol. 3, p. 29, no. 19

The text was added to this fifteenth-century manuscript made in Flanders for English use, probably still in the fifteenth century, in England. It links contemplation of Christ's sufferings, numbered as five (see notes preceding **3** above), with prayers for salvation; at the end it asks for deliverance at the hour of death. In the fourth section the words were either composed or adapted for the use of a woman.

1 Lord Jesus Christ, I adore you as you hang on the Cross with the crown of thorns on your head. I pray that your Cross may deliver me from the avenging angel.
*Our father*
*Hail Mary*

2 Lord Jesus Christ, I adore you, wounded on the Cross, given gall and vinegar to drink. I pray that your wounds may be my soul's salvation.
*Our father*
*Hail Mary*

3 Lord Jesus Christ, I adore you as you are laid in the tomb and anointed with spices. I pray that your death may be the life of my soul.
*Our father*
*Hail Mary*

4 Lord Jesus Christ, good shepherd, preserve the just, make sinners righteous, have pity on all the faithful and be merciful to me, a sinful woman.
*Our father*
*Hail Mary*

5 Lord Jesus Christ, by the bitter suffering you bore for me on the Cross, most of all when your very noble soul departed from your body, have mercy on my soul in its parting. Amen
*Our father*
*Hail Mary*

*Forty-six thousand and twenty years and fifty-three days of pardon*

### 9.3 Agnes Hykeley's prayer

*O altissima humanitas*
Agnes Hykeley's Hours
Cambridge University Library MS Dd.15.19, fol. 158v
English rubric + Latin prayer

Ref.: for the cult and incipient feast of the Five Wounds, see Pfaff 1970, 84–91

The text was added at the end of the manuscript, perhaps in Agnes Hykeley's own hand. The writing is similar to a request for prayer and her signature, as found in the top and bottom margins of fol. 5v: 'Good Mystrys in your prayers Remember hyr that wrote thys . . . Agnes Hykeley'.

*To all those who daily say the following prayer with true devotion before an image of the crucifix, are granted by indulgence as many days of pardon as there are pebbles in the sea and blades of grass growing on the earth*

O most exalted human flesh and innocent blood, O great suffering, O torment of Christ, O deep wounds, O piercing by the lance, O flowing of blood, O breaking of the heart, O venerable grace of God, help me to attain eternal life. Amen

**9.4 Eleanor Worcester's prayer**

*Most wysest lady*

Eleanor Worcester's Hours

British Library, MS Harley 1251, fols 182r–v

Middle English salutations with repetition of Latin *Ave Maria*

There are comparable invocations in British Library, MS Harley 494, fols 84v–85r. In the Bridgettine compilation Lambeth Palace Library MS 546, fols 7v–20v, fifteen such invocations are expanded into complex prayers dwelling on the Fifteen Sorrows of Mary. Eleanor Worcester's salutations are remarkable for the commentary which follows them, in which a rather frivolous manner of fulfilling the requirements of the indulgence comes to the fore, as noted above (p. 17). If a person cannot remember the ten virtues of the Blessed Virgin (and it is hard to imagine that the virtues, especially the third virtue, poverty, will have appealed to this suppliant), she should just say 'Hail Mary' while bearing the ten virtues (whatever they may be) in mind. One should also bring to mind the five principal Joys. Wearing in one's girdle a scroll with the salutations and virtues inscribed on it will also earn a few days release from purgatory.

Most wise lady, [*Hail Mary*]
Most chaste lady, [*Hail Mary*]
Most poor lady, [*Hail Mary*]
Most lovely lady, [*Hail Mary*]
Most gracious lady, [*Hail Mary*]
Most obedient lady, [*Hail Mary*]

Most patient lady, [*Hail Mary*]
Most pure lady, [*Hail Mary*]
Most meek lady, [*Hail Mary*]
Most sorrowful lady, *Hail Mary*

Every time you say these ten *Hail Marys* and remember these ten virtues you have ten thousand years of pardon, and for every day on which you carry it in your girdle, forty days of pardon. You do not need to remember them one by one, but you say 'I greet you with the same greeting with which the angel Gabriel greeted you,' saying *Hail Mary* in worship of her ten virtues, even though you do not know which they are. And also you must add to them the five principal joys, the Annunciation, Nativity, Resurrection, Ascension and Assumption. The pardon is for 10,000 years and 10,000 days; and the wearing in the girdle ten days.

*Hail Mary*

## 10 Salutations to the Blessed Virgin Mary

**10.1** *Ave seinte Marie mere al creatur*

De Brailes Hours

British Library, Additional MS 49999, fols 102v–104v

All or part also in eight further manuscripts, contemporary with or later than BL Additional MS 49999, none of which is a book of hours

Anglo-Norman verse

Refs: Dean and Boulton 2000, no. 740; Donovan 1991

This vernacular text was added to the standard Latin contents of the De Brailes Hours before it was bound, presumably at the behest of the young lady patron shown in miniatures. Just as the text of the Hours of the Virgin in this earliest surviving English book of hours is interwoven with images of Christ's suffering and Passion, so also this additional poem celebrating Mary is in part christological: the devotee contemplates Mary and Jesus together. The text is rich in biblical Marian imagery. From interpretations of Old Testament texts as prophesying the birth and life of Mary come the salutation to her as rod of Jesse (verse 2) and many further nature images of flower, rose, rosebush, sun, star, light; tower of David (verse 3), temple of Solomon (verse 4) and further architectural and decorative images of throne, sealed window, shining glass, chandelier, gateway of the Saviour, marble chamber, stairway of paradise; from the New Testament gospels and Acts of the Apostles come the salutations of Mary as virgin mother of God (verses 6 and 18), who bore her father (verse 6), was mother of Jesus (verse 15), and virgin of the Annunciation (verse 21), illumined by the Holy Spirit (verses 21 and 23), illuminer of the early church (verse 20).

From apocryphal miracle narratives comes the rescue of the sinful bishop Theophilus (verse 22). Jesus, too, is flower, rose, brightness, lightbringer, and sun. He is also the stone through which Goliath died (verse 3) in the Old Testament narrative of David and Goliath; the harrower of hell (verse 6).

Most of the other manuscripts continue this text with a full litany of the saints. It is possible that the scribe of BL Additional MS 49999 ran out of space for this late addition, and therefore omitted the litany; the writing gets smaller and the whole text is more compressed towards the end.

1 Hail holy Mary, mother of the creator,
Queen of angels and path full of gentleness;
Hail star of the sea, shining so gloriously,
Stairway to paradise, the sinner's salvation.

2 Hail holy Mary, rod of king Jesse,
From you spread the flower which is full of bounty,
Of power, of vigour and of humility,
Of counsel, of holiness and mercy,
And of the fear of God which checkmates the devil.
Glorious queen, have mercy on me.

3 Hail tower of king David, hail holy Mary,
From you came the stone through which Goliath died,
And Adam's descendants returned from death to life;
Have mercy on me, sweet beloved.

4 Hail holy Mary, who are the temple of Solomon,
To you came the angel whose name is Gabriel;
He descended to you gently in great love,
To save his people from the cruel enemy.
*Our father*
*Hail Mary*

5 Hail holy Mary, mother of king Jesus,
Source of joy and path of salvation;
Protect me from all evils and from the devil of perdition,
Draw me away from hell, which is hateful.

6 Hail holy Mary, who made Adam so joyful,
And all the people whom the devil had ensnared;
Just as they were brought back by you from sorrow,
Have mercy on me through your great pity.
*Our father*
*Hail Mary*

7 Hail holy Mary, glorious mother,
Precious virgin who bore your father;

Have mercy on all sinners,
Protect my body and my soul from my adversary.
*Our father*
*Hail Mary*

8 Hail holy Mary, hail glorious one,
Hail queen of heaven, hail precious one,
Hail mother of Jesus, hail bride of God,
Sweet lady, amend my wretched life.
*Our father*
*Hail Mary*

9 Hail holy Mary, full of gentleness,
Have mercy on me, flower of womankind,
So that through my folly I may not be brought to sorrow,
Where there is pain without end and tears and sadness.
*Our father*
*Hail Mary*

10 Hail holy Mary, helping queen,
Flower of all the world, wonder of angels;
As your gentleness, my lady, grants protection,
Ask your dear son to be merciful to me.
*Our father*
*Hail Mary*

11 Hail holy Mary, who bore the brightness
Which none born of woman can contemplate,
Before the severing of body and soul,
Let me be acquitted of my sin.

12 Hail holy Mary, who bore the flower
From which the day received its light,
Sun and moon their splendour;
Have mercy on me through your great gentleness.
*Our father*
*Hail Mary*

13 Hail holy Mary, brightly shining rose,
Flower of all the world enclosed in virginity,
Hail the holy meekness resting in you,
In heaven and earth there is nothing so sweet.
*Our father*
*Hail Mary*

14 Hail holy Mary, meekest of all women,
Give me, my lady, power and goodness,
Abstinence and peace, love and chastity,
And by your gentle grace, holy charity

Through which I may abandon sin in this world.
*Our father*
*Hail Mary*

15 Hail throne of Jesus, hail holy Mary,
Have pity on all who cry to you for mercy,
While they lead wretched lives in this world;
Exert your power so that God does not forget us,
And we may deserve his holy help;
And the joy of heaven, may God grant it to us.
*Our father*
*Hail Mary*

16 Hail holy Mary, brightly shining sun,
Mother of our Lord, Jesus the almighty;
Those who were in sorrow, bring to great joy
And Lucifer to flames, the proud tyrant.

17 Hail holy Mary, glorious queen,
Joy of womankind, virgin crown;
Ask your sweet son to whom the world bows down
To give me a remedy for all my sins.
*Our father*
*Hail Mary*

18 Hail holy Mary, rich rose bush,
From you came the peerless blossom;
We can marvel at this gentle rose
That deigned to live on earth.

19 Hail holy Mary, brightly shining glass,
Jesus, light of the world, descended to you;
As virgin you received him and remained a virgin,
As we well know from holy scripture.
*Our father*
*Hail Mary*

20 Hail holy Mary, who bore the lion
Who is more gentle than any dove;
And by his great strength he overcame the dragon
To deliver his people from infernal prison.
*Our father*
*Hail Mary*

21 Hail holy Mary, glorious chandelier,
It was God's will to illumine holy church with you,
And send out his messengers throughout the world
To teach life to the people.

*Our father*
*Hail Mary*

22 Hail holy Mary, queen illumined
By the sun's descent into you, the deity;
When the angel Gabriel said to you 'Hail Mary'
You were illumined by the Holy Spirit.

23 Hail holy Mary, full of pity,
As appeared in Theophilus who had denied God;
He paid homage to the devil and confirmed it with his blood,
You returned the charter that was carried to hell.

24 Hail holy Mary, sealed window,
You are raised up above all things;
Hail, illumined by the Holy Spirit,
Have mercy on me, crowned queen.

25 Hail holy Mary, gateway of the Saviour,
Through you he came into the world to take away sorrow,
In you, lady, he found the flower of virginity,
Have mercy on me through your great gentleness.

26 Hail holy Mary, marble chamber,
In you the sun that never sets descended
To deliver the orphaned people from hell;
Have mercy on me, glorious queen.

27 Glorious queen, mother of the creator,
Hear my prayer through your great gentleness;
For those who have honoured me in this world,
Give them that joy where there will be no toil.

28 Again I pray, my lady, by your humility,
Have mercy on me by holy Charity;
Give them in this world power and virtue
So that they may live according to your will.

29 Those who have passed from this world to sorrow
And are in purgatory, in travail for their sin,
Give them your sweet help, my lady,
To live with your dear son in great gentleness.

30 I never heard, my lady, of any sinner
Who wanted to abandon his sin for love of you,
And asked your help, but that your help was granted;
Have mercy on me by your great gentleness.
*Our father*
*Hail Mary*

31 Since I was seven years old I never stopped sinning,
Since my bad flesh would never cease;
Glorious queen, I ask your help,
You who can light up all the world with joy.

**10.2** *Ave et gaude*

Carew-Poyntz Hours

Cambridge, Fitzwilliam Museum MS 48, fols 58v–82r

Latin prose

Shortened version in the Neville of Hornby Hours, British Library MS Egerton 2781, fols 9r–20v, 24r. The gathering containing the final words of the *Ave et gaude* salutations in this manuscript has been folded, or bound, wrongly, so that the final words of the text are dislocated from their proper place. The leaves now numbered as fols 24–27 should follow fol. 20, preceding the leaves now numbered as fols 21–23. The dislocation also leads to apparent lack of continuity in several other texts.

Refs: James 1895, 100–120; Sandler 1986, Vol. 2, no. 130, 143–145; Smith 2003, esp. 184–90 for the shorter text, and plate 6, figs 84, 187, 190, 192, 258, 275 for reproductions of miniatures from British Library MS Egerton 2781 (mis-folding or mis-binding of fols 21r–27v not noted in Smith Appendix 4); Wilmart 1932, 328 n. 1 for the shorter text from MS Egerton 2781

The forty-seven salutations are accompanied throughout by beautiful illustrations, in both manuscripts. In the Fitzwilliam manuscript, following the first salutation, which is longer than the others and occupies a full page with its illustration, there are usually two salutations with accompanying illustrations on each page. In the Egerton manuscript there is usually one salutation with accompanying illustration. In the Fitzwilliam manuscript one leaf has been lost following salutation 20 (between fols 68 and 69 on present numbering); it is likely that the original number of salutations was around fifty. The shortened version in the Egerton manuscript unfortunately does not contain any of the missing salutations, although complete on its own terms.

The first salutation is built on the Hail Mary; in order to make this visible, the words of the Hail Mary are italicised in the translation. The subsequent salutations take the reader or viewer through the entire sequence of Marian life-story narratives, from apocryphal as well as biblical sources. Both the long and the short versions of the text have the salutations pertaining to Mary's Nativity, Presentation, Annunciation + Conception, Dormition or Death, Assumption + Coronation. Again, both the long and the short versions have the salutation to her as the only one whose belief never faltered, on the Saturday after Good Friday, preceding Christ's Resurrection on Easter Sunday (**10.2** 36).

1 *Hail* and rejoice, virgin *Mary*; merciful, gentle and holy path through this wretched human life, *full of* all virtue and *grace*, virgin mild above all virgins, save me .N. at the hour of death from the pain of hell.
*The Lord is with you*. Today, I beseech you, be with me so that I may know and feel and rejoice with you.
*Blessed are you* surrounded by the lordship of heaven *among women* and in your most pure womb, *and*
*Blessed is the fruit* created by the adumbration of the Holy Spirit, who destroyed the sorrows inflicted by Eve and the grief of the blessed fruit *of your womb*.
*Hail Mary*
*Hail Mary*

2 Hail and rejoice, virgin Mary, of the seed of Abraham and the tribe of Judah and the royal progeny of David in holy procession.
*Hail Mary*

3 Hail and rejoice, virgin Mary, who through your holy birth heralded joy to the world beyond words.
*Hail Mary*

4 Hail and rejoice, virgin Mary; offered by your parents to the temple of the lord, you ascended the steps quickly with no-one to guide you, beyond the strength of one of your age.
*Hail Mary*

5 Hail and rejoice, virgin Mary, who by your holy life illuminated the church of Christ throughout the world.
*Hail Mary*

6 Hail and rejoice, virgin Mary, you who, brought up in the temple of God, were first singularly pleasing to God through your peerless wish for perpetual virginity.
*Hail Mary*

7 Hail and rejoice, virgin Mary, you who were willing to live in concord with righteous Joseph as husband and guardian, assigned to you by the angel.
*Hail Mary*

8 Hail and rejoice, blessed virgin Mary, who gave credence to the words of the archangel Gabriel without doubting.
*Hail Mary*

9 Hail and rejoice, virgin Mary, who with your humble consent truly conceived the son of God in your womb.
*Hail Mary*

10 Hail and rejoice, virgin Mary, who through the greeting of your blessed lips brought joy alike to Elizabeth and John.
*Hail Mary*

11 Hail and rejoice, chosen virgin and mother Mary, who gave birth without pain from your virginal flesh to God and man in one.
*Hail Mary*

12 Hail and rejoice, virgin and mother Mary, who, through your fecundity in giving birth and maintaining your virginity intact, transcended the curse of the Old Testament.
*Hail Mary*

13 Hail and rejoice, virgin mother Mary, who revealed to the shepherds little Jesus wrapped in swaddling clothes, lying in the crib.
*Hail Mary*

14 Hail and rejoice, virgin and mother Mary, who amply suckled the son of God and saviour of the world with your virginal breasts, filled with milk from heaven.
*Hail Mary*

15 Hail and rejoice, mother Mary, who laudably remained an untouched virgin before, during and after giving birth.
*Hail Mary*

16 Hail and rejoice, virgin and mother Mary, who alone opposed all the heresies in the world.
*Hail Mary*

17 Hail and rejoice, virgin and mother Mary, who kindly showed your son Jesus to the three kings when they came to adore him.
*Hail Mary*

18 Hail and rejoice, wisest virgin and mother Mary, who understood the spiritual meaning of the mystical gifts offered to your son.
*Hail Mary*

19 Hail and rejoice, virgin and mother Mary, who secretly fled to Egypt from the malice of Herod with your innocent son, and with Joseph, alerted by the angel.
*Hail Mary*

20 Hail and rejoice, virgin and mother Mary, who, advised by the angel, after Herod's death faithfully brought your son back to the land of Israel.
*Hail Mary*

21 Hail and rejoice, virgin and mother Mary, who rejoiced at finding

your son after three days sitting amidst the doctors, and patiently listened to his irreproachable answer to your admonishment.
*Hail Mary*

22 Hail and rejoice, virgin and mother Mary, who, summoned to the marriage at Cana in Galilee with Jesus, hastened to carry out whatever instructions he gave.
*Hail Mary*

23 Hail and rejoice, virgin and mother Mary who, reporting to your son the lack of wine, saw the abundance of best wine made by him from water poured out of six jars.
*Hail Mary*

24 Hail and rejoice, virgin and mother Mary, who firmly showed your faith before all others in the further miraculous deeds of your son.
*Hail Mary*

25 Hail and rejoice, virgin and mother Mary, who stored in your memory your son's parables and comparisons, keeping them in your heart.
*Hail Mary*

26 Hail and rejoice, virgin and mother Mary, who with wisdom beheld the divinity of your son in his humanity, on the occasions when he restored Lazarus to life, and when he walked on the water.
*Hail Mary*

27 Hail and rejoice, virgin and mother Mary, who, seeing Jesus seated on an ass and coming to his Passion in Jerusalem, recognised the fulfilment of the prophets' prediction.
*Hail Mary*

28 Hail and rejoice, virgin Mary, who cherished the mediator between God and men even more fervently than others did, when the believing Jews cried 'Hosanna' to him.
*Hail Mary*

29 Hail and rejoice, virgin and mother Mary, who recorded ineradicably in your heart the example of profound humility given by your son when he washed the feet of his disciples.
*Hail Mary*

30 Hail and rejoice, virgin and mother Mary, who recognised that when the apostles were fed with Christ's body, taken from you, and his blood, they were receiving salvation.
*Hail Mary*

31 Hail and rejoice, virgin and mother Mary, who vehemently abhorred

the malice of the Jews, and the avarice of the betrayer, when your son was arrested.
*Hail Mary*

32 Hail and rejoice, virgin Mary and mother, who soothingly bandaged the pierced hands and feet of your son.
*Hail Mary*

33 Hail, most holy lady, who, when you were commended as virgin to the virgin [St John the Evangelist] from the Cross, with desolation acknowledged the servant in place of the lord, the disciple in place of the master, John in place of your son.
*Hail Mary*

34 Hail and rejoice, most holy lady Mary, whose soul was cruelly pierced with the sword of bitterest sorrow as your son died for the salvation of mankind.
*Hail Mary*

35 Hail and rejoice, most holy lady, ever-virgin Mary, who beheld water and blood gushing forth when Jesus's side was pierced with the lance.
*Hail Mary*

36 Hail and rejoice, most holy lady, virgin Mary, who alone remained constant in the faith of the church on Holy Saturday, when the apostles wavered.
*Hail Mary*

37 Hail and rejoice, most holy lady, ever-virgin Mary, who truly renewed your joy on the third day when your son arose from the darkness of death to life.
*Hail Mary*

38 Hail and rejoice, most holy lady, ever-virgin Mary, who joyfully and reverently received him as he returned triumphant from hell and the devil.
*Hail Mary*

39 Hail and rejoice, most devoted ever-virgin Mary, who persevered in unanimous prayer with the apostles and the holy women, awaiting the fulfilment of the promise after the Ascension of Lord Jesus.
*Hail Mary*

40 Hail and rejoice in celebration of the true Resurrection, you who welcomed with delight the manifold appearances of your son for forty days.
*Hail Mary*

41 Hail and rejoice, ever-virgin Mary, who with your blessed eyes saw your son Jesus miraculously ascending to heaven.
*Hail Mary*

42 Hail and rejoice, most holy mother and ever-virgin Mary, who patently opened for us the gate of paradise that had been closed to all by Eve.
*Hail Mary*

43 Hail and rejoice, most holy ever-virgin Mary, who spoke familiarly with the apostles and other believers concerning the incarnation and birth of Christ.
*Hail Mary*

44 Hail and rejoice, most holy lady, ever-virgin Mary, who felt within you most vibrantly the sweetness of the Holy Spirit's love, visibly descending upon you and the apostles.
*Hail Mary*

45 Hail and rejoice, most holy lady, ever-virgin and mother Mary, most happy of all living creatures, who, at the consummation of your most pure life, spiritually commended your most blessed soul to the hands of your beloved son.
*Hail Mary*

46 Hail and rejoice, most holy lady, ever-virgin Mary, who, taken up into heaven, were most deservedly welcomed by all the saints, exalted above the rank of the angels, and set upon the throne beside your son.
*Hail Mary*

47 Hail and rejoice, most excellent queen of heaven, lady of angels and archangels, mediator between God and man, who alone through God have sufficiently confirmed us in every truth of the faith.
*Hail Mary*

**10.3** *Ave ancilla trinitatis*

Syon Abbey Hours

Syon Abbey MS 2, fol. 126r

Latin

Ref.: For St Bridget's representation of Mary, see Graef 1963, 309–310

In the Bridgettine night Office, *Sermo angelicus de virginis excellentia*, St Bridget presents Mary as Mother of Wisdom illumining ignorance, asserts her presence in divine thought before the creation of the world, and in the thought of angels and Old Testament patriarchs, and traces her life from birth to the Assumption. Some of these ideas are found here in this brief celebration.

Hail maiden of the Trinity, hail bride of the Holy Spirit,
Hail mother of our Lord Jesus Christ, hail sister of angels,
Hail promise of the prophets, Hail queen of the patriarchs,
Hail teacher of the evangelists, hail learned adviser of the apostles,
Hail comforter of martyrs, Hail wellspring and joy of confessors,
Hail adornment of virgins, hail consoler of the living and the dead,
Be with me in all tribulation and perils.

## 11 Little Psalter of Our Lady

*En le honuraunce duz sire Jhesu*

Norwich Hours

Norwich Castle Museum 158.926/4f., fols 145r–149v

Also in the De Mohun Hours, Boston Public Library MS 124, fols 103r–105r; and in the Percy Hours, British Library MS Harley 1260, fols 188r–191r

Anglo-Norman French rubrics, headings and verse prayers to Jesus, then Mary; alternating with Latin verse prayers to the deity. Italics are used in the translation for the Anglo-Norman rubrics and headings, and for the Latin prayers; roman print for the Anglo-Norman verse prayers

Ref.: Dean and Boulton 2000, no. 758

This 'little psalter' combines invocations by the five Joys of Mary (Annunciation + Conception, Nativity, Resurrection, Ascension, Assumption + Coronation) with verses and responses, prayers to God, and the recitation fifty times of 'Hail Mary'. The prayers to God are the same as in those used in the Lyte Hours acrostic sequence (see **3** above).

*Here begins the little psalter of our lady in French and in Latin, and it contains only fifty times Hail Mary, and whoever says it every day will receive the blessing of holy Mary at the hour of death*

1 *The first Joy, of the Conception*

In honour, sweet Lord Jesus, of that most holy 'Hail'
By which the angel greeted your mother on earth,
Who conceived you within her body for our salvation,
Hear my prayer for that great humility.

O lady, for the great Joy that you conceived in your heart,
Help me to attain grace in this world,
And to praise your Conception in such a way

That I may keep my soul from sin.

O mother of Jesus, fountain of mercy,
He who made us all took flesh from you, to deliver us from pain.

*Our father*. Once.
*Hail Mary*. Ten times

Verse
*Pray for us, holy mother of God,*
Response
*So that we may be made worthy of the promises of Christ.*

Prayer. *Deus qui respiciens humilitatem ancille tue*
[as in text **3**, 1]

2 *The second Joy, of the Nativity of her son*

In honour, sweet Lord Jesus, of your Nativity,
When you deigned to be born of the maid in your humanity,
Hear me pray to you by that fraternity,
So that I am not disinherited from your joy.

O Mary, for the great joy you had at that hour,
When you saw him born of you without pain or blemish,
To redeem us all from pain and filth,
Help me to remember this as long as I live.

O Mary, remember why he was born of you,
And you will be advocate for me and all sinners.

*Our father*. Once
*Hail Mary*. Ten times

Verse
*Pray for us, holy mother of God,*
Response
*So that we may be made worthy of the promises of Christ.*

Prayer. *Deus qui sine materno dolore in lucem prodiens*
[as in text **3**, 2]

3 *The third Joy of our lady, of the Resurrection*

In honour, sweet Lord Jesus, of your Resurrection to life,
When you appeared in glory to your mother Mary,
To gladden her heart, and all the company,
Help me before death so that my soul does not perish.

O Mary, full of joy at his Resurrection,
Pray for me, that I may so conduct myself in this life

That I may greet your son with grace,
And enter into your glory on the Day of Judgement.

Help me, Mary, on that terrible day,
So that I do not suffer pain or sorrow for my sins.

*Our father*. Once
*Hail Mary*. Ten times

Verse
*Pray for us, holy mother of God,*
Response
*So that we may be made worthy of the promises of Christ.*

Prayer. *Deus qui in cruce moriens matris dolorem*
[as in text **3**, 3]

4 *The fourth Joy of our lady, for the Ascension of her son*

In honour, sweet Lord Jesus, of your Ascension,
When you ascended to heaven in procession,
Help me to ascend there with your blessing,
So that I receive neither a place in hell, nor your malediction.

O Mary, for the great joy you felt when you saw him
Ascending, and he promised the Holy Spirit to everyone there,
Help me so that I may come to his joy,
And see and behold him in that joy without end.

O Mary, crowned queen of humility,
Help me to ascend there to see his humanity.

*Our father*. Once
*Hail Mary*. Ten times

Verse
*Pray for us, holy mother of God,*
Response
*So that we may be made worthy of the promises of Christ.*

Prayer. *Deus qui gaudium matris tue te ascendente*
[as in text **3**, 4]

5 *The fifth Joy of our lady, of the Assumption*

In honour, sweet Lord Jesus, of the Assumption,
When you vested your mother in her magnificence
And let her reign with you as queen of glory,
Help me come to her and rejoice with her joy.

O Mary, sweet lady, queen of grace on earth,

Receive these Aves from me and let them please you.
I offer them to you for my sins; let me withdraw from my sins
So that I may praise you for ever as maid and mother.

O Mary, I know no help but to pray for your grace,
That you may help me come to gentle Jesus, and behold his face without end.
Amen

*Our father*. Once
*Hail Mary*. Ten times

Verse
*Pray for us, holy mother of God,*
Response
*So that we may be made worthy of the promises of Christ.*

Prayer. *Deus qui beatam virginem Mariam super choros*
[as in text **3**, 5]

## 12 Verse prayers by the Joys of Mary

### 12.1 The Joys and Honours of Mary

*Douce dame jo vus pri*

DuBois Hours

New York, Pierpont Morgan Library MS M. 700, fols 131v–136r

Also in the Harnhull Psalter-Hours (Stratton-on-the-Fosse, Downside Abbey MS 26533, fols 7v–8v), with Latin 'Our father' and 10 x 'Hail Mary' following each verse

Anglo-Norman verses, + Latin *Ave Maria* 'Hail Mary'

Ref.: Dean and Boulton 2000, no. 769

This is very much a woman's prayer, with its strong focus on the Christ child, especially on the lactation (verses 6–8), and on the cradling of Christ (verses 9 and 10). Verse 11 returns to the incarnation, already 'hailed' in verse 2. The last third of the prayer moves more rapidly through Resurrection (verse 13), Ascension (verse 14), Pentecost (verse 15) and Assumption (verse 16).

1 Sweet lady, I pray you,
Humbly I beg your mercy,
For the honour God showed you
When he sent you his angel –
When Gabriel announced this to you,
Brought you the message,

And spoke the sweet salutation to you,
That Jesus would be enclosed within you –
For the joy that you had then,
When you conceived the son of God,
I pray you, sweet lady,
Hear my prayer.
*Hail Mary*

2 Sweet lady, queen of heaven,
Mother of God, virgin maid,
I beg you for the honour
That God, our Lord, showed you
When our Lord Jesus Christ
Became incarnate within you,
Listen and be ready,
And hear my request.
*Hail Mary*

3 Gentle lady, I beg you,
Very humbly I pray you,
For the joy and the honour
You had at his birth,
Hasten, my lady,
To give me joy for my prayer.
*Hail Mary*

4 Gentle lady St Mary,
Our help, our aid,
I beg you very softly,
For the honour of the descent
Of the Holy Ghost, casting its shadow
As it lodged within you,
Hear my prayer
And grant my request.
*Hail Mary*

5 Gentle lady St Mary,
Full of God's grace,
For the honour God showed you
When you saw Jesus newborn,
Lady, grant this boon
And hear my prayer.
*Hail Mary*

6 Sweet lady, for the honour
You had that day
When you suckled the son of God –
With your breasts you loved him greatly –

I beg you by your delight
To grant my desire.
*Hail Mary*

7 Glorious sweet lady,
Precious mother of God,
For the honour God showed you
When he took nourishment from you –
Blessed is the right breast
And blessed the left –
Hear my prayer, lady,
And what I desire.
*Hail Mary*

8 Sweet lady, sweet queen,
Sweet mother, sweet maid,
For the honour of the sweet milk
Your creator sucked,
I beg you, dear lady,
To hear my prayer.
*Hail Mary*

9 Sweet lady, I beg you,
Praying as best I can,
For the honour of the embrace
And the joy of clasping
Your dear son, that you felt
When you held him in your arms,
Grant me true pardon
And hear my prayer.
*Hail Mary*

10 Gentle lady St Mary,
I, your maidservant, pray you
For the honour of the God you loved
When you laid him in his cradle,
And covered him with kisses,
And for the joy it brought you,
I beseech you, virgin Mary,
That my prayer be heard.
*Hail Mary*

11 Gentle lady Mary,
Handmaid and beloved of God,
I beg you by the honour
That God our creator showed you
When he sent his son, Jesus Christ,
And took flesh in your body –

That blessed body was our salvation
When he became incarnate for our sake –
Just as truly, hear my prayer;
I implore you, sweet lady.
*Hail Mary*

12 Sweet lady, I pray you,
Humbly I beg your mercy,
For that joy, for that honour,
When you presented our Lord
In the temple – that was Jesus Christ –
And Simeon took him in his arms,
Just as truly, dear virgin,
Grant my prayer.
*Hail Mary*

13 Sweet lady, may God hear you
For that honour, for the joy
That you had when your son
Rose from death to life, I pray;
Preserve my body from danger,
My soul from deadly exile,
And my relations and my friends;
Help the dead and the living,
And make haste to grant me
My prayer and my desire.
*Hail Mary*

14 Sweet lady St Mary,
Mother of Jesus, mother of life,
For that joy, for the honour
You had on that day
When you saw Jesus Christ
With that flesh he took within you
Ascend aloft to heaven on high,
The son of God who came to save us,
Grant me just as truly
My prayer, now quickly.
*Hail Mary*

15 Sweet lady, blessed virgin,
Mother of God, queen of heaven,
I ask you and implore
Your grace as my lady,
For that joy and deep awareness
You felt without doubt
When your son sent to you
And to several apostles

The Holy Spirit, the Paraclete,
And they were comforted,
I pray you, sweet lady,
Hear my prayer.
*Hail Mary*

16 Sweet lady, mother of Jesus Christ,
For the honour God showed you
When you left this world
So full of adversity –
You ascended truly to heaven,
And festively your son
Seated you on the holy throne
And made you queen of heaven –
Listen and be ready,
Lady, to hear my request.
*Hail Mary*

17 Sweet lady, sweet queen,
Sweet mother, sweet maid,
Sweet daughter, sweet mother,
God is your son, God is your father;
I pray you by the honours,
By the joys, the delights
God accorded you on this earth –
It is right that I seek your grace –
Have mercy on me
And on my loved ones, I pray.
Defend my body from shame,
Wherever I may be,
And grant me confession
And true pardon of my sins.
Amen

## 12.2 The Five Joys + celestial joy

*Duce dame seinte Marie*

DuBois Hours

New York, Pierpont Morgan Library MS M.700, fols 136r–137v

Anglo-Norman rubric and verse

Ref.: Dean and Boulton 2000, no. 759

The Five Joys of Mary's earthly life – in this case, Annunciation (+ Conception), Nativity, Miracle at Cana, Resurrection and Ascension – are followed here by a sixth 'celestial joy', when Mary is in heaven. The rubric guaranteeing the value of the prayer to be found true, within a fortnight, suggests that this text was one to be used in time of trouble (see also **22.2**,

**23**). The last verse, with its reference to the miracle of the unchaste abbess (see p. 15 above), makes it especially suitable for a suppliant troubled by sins of the flesh.

*Do not neglect on any account to say this prayer every day two or three times, if you can, in front of the image of our lady St Mary; and I promise you that this will be of more value than anything else you can say, and you will find this true within a fortnight*

1 Sweet lady St Mary
Who bore the king of life,
You conceived him through the Holy Spirit
When Gabriel spoke the salutations to you –
Truly he greeted you justly
When he came from God in heaven –
Lady, with great joy you conceived him;
You rejoice now, you rejoiced then,
And certainly without end will be
The joy you have received.
By the joy, blessed mother,
Which was yours and which remains,
In your son the sovereign king,
Lady, remember me.

2 And for the immense joy you had
At the birth of your sweet child,
Joy, in looking after the blessed one,
In feeding him and nursing him;

3 And for the great joy that came to you
When he made good wine out of water –
For this joy and these honours,
Raise me up from my sorrows.

4 And for the joy and love
You experienced through the son of God
When he was resurrected from death –
Great was the joy and comfort
You had, lady, in truth
When he was resurrected from death –
He revealed himself to you, my lady,
When he came back to life from death;
By that love and that joy
Set me, lady, on the right path.

5 And by the great joy you had
When your son ascended into heaven
With the flesh he received

From you, lady, as it pleased him;

6 Sweet lady who on earth knew
These joys, and then received
The joy which is everlasting,
Which certainly will be eternally yours –
By these joys, blessed mother,
Pray your son, pray your father,
That he grant me true pardon
And remission of my sins,
And give me the sustenance I need,
And, if it please him, meek heart and good will,
And defend me from harm;
And this, lady, I devotedly pray.

7 Sweet glorious virgin,
Blessed precious mother,
Remember the pity
You showed to the pregnant abbess
When the nun denounced her
Whom she had found and fed;
Pray your son, pray your father,
Who on the Cross addressed you as mother
And commended you to his beloved disciple,
To have mercy on me, a sinful woman,
And grant me to lead such a life
That he may receive my soul.
Amen

### 12.3 The Fifteen Joys

*Douce dame seinte Marie*

DuBois Hours

New York, Pierpont Morgan Library MS M.700, fols 137v–141r

Anglo-Norman prose rubric and text, Latin canticles

Ref.: Dean and Boulton 2000, no. 769

This is a more learned and sophisticated composition than the two preceding texts. There was a tradition of linking Joys or Sorrows with virtues or vices in complex verse or prose structures. Here, each Joy is linked to a virtue. The fifteen sections are structured in three sets of five; sections 5, 10 and 15 are followed by a canticle, 'Our father' and 'Hail Mary', rather in the manner of a liturgical text. The matching of Joys and Sorrows with virtues and vices was strongly developed some decades later than this particular text in Bridgettine devotions (see, for instance, British

Library MS Harley 494, fols 85v–88v; Lambeth Palace Library MS 546, fols 7v–20v).

*Here begin the fifteen joys of our sweet lady St Mary with the fifteen virtues which are drawn from the holy gospel; and then the canticle* Blessed is the Lord. *All the canticle is to be said with* Glory to the father; *then afterwards* Our father *and* Hail Mary

1 *The first joy is this:*
Sweet lady St Mary, for the joy that you had in the glorious message that St Gabriel announced to you – that the son of God was to be born of you – and for the blessed humility that you showed when you answered 'Behold me here, the handmaiden of God', beseech your dear son, our sweet Lord Jesus Christ, to give us true humility.
*Hail Mary*

2 Sweet lady St Mary, for the joy that you had when St Elizabeth, filled with the Holy Spirit, with her blessed lips firmly acclaimed you the most blessed among women, everlasting virgin, mother of chastity, beseech your sweet son, Jesus Christ our Lord, to grant us true chastity.
*Hail Mary*

3 Sweet lady St Mary, for the joy that you had when the son of God was born of you without pain or blemish, and you laid him in the manger wrapped in thin cloth because there was nowhere else in that tiny little dwelling, according to the testimony of the shepherds who adored him, beseech your dear son, sweet Jesus Christ our Lord, to grant us true poverty, and let us cherish scorn and deprivation for his love, who deigned to become small and poor for our love.
*Hail Mary*

4 Sweet lady St Mary, for the joy that you had when the star appeared above the little dwelling and the three kings came from the East and adored your son, and offered him myrrh and incense and more than the heart can imagine – they rejoiced in your simplicity – beseech your dear sweet son, our Lord Jesus Christ, to grant us true simplicity.
*Hail Mary*

5 Sweet lady St Mary, for the joy that you had when you presented your dear sweet son our Lord Jesus Christ [in the temple] and St Simeon and St Anne received him and testified to all the people that he had come, true saviour of the people and true light to all nations, beseech him to illumine our hearts so that we may truly acknowledge him, and may he give us true wisdom.
Amen

*Canticle. Magnificat* [as in text **1**, canticle at vespers]
*Our father*
*Hail Mary*

6 Sweet lady St Mary, for the great joy that you had when the angel warned your husband St Joseph that he should flee from the search which the cruel king Herod was undertaking for your dear son our Lord Jesus, and for your patience in exile when you were far from your country in the dark, and remained fugitives there and banished for seven years, and especially for the consolation you had when the angel said you should return to your country, and those who sought the child were dead, beseech your dear sweet son, our Lord Jesus Christ, to make us worthy to suffer a part of the noble Passion he suffered for us, and to grant us patience and comfort in the adversities of this life.
*Hail Mary*

7 Sweet lady St Mary, for the joy you had when you found your sweet son in the temple disputing with the masters of the law, and especially when he returned with you to Nazareth and was obedient to you, full of grace and knowledge before God and the people, beseech him to give us true obedience towards him, and towards those whom we are bound to obey for his love.
*Hail Mary*

8 Sweet lady St Mary, for the joy you had in the miracles of your sweet son, especially when he turned water into wine at your request and revealed his glory – that he was true God and born of you, a virgin – beseech him to grant us holy truth in our words and deeds and thoughts.
*Hail Mary*

9 Sweet lady St Mary, for the ardent and stable love you felt when you followed your sweet son to the Cross and saw with your blessed eyes how he was tortured, and, mopping his brow, saw him suffer so much – who could so easily have delivered himself – beseech him to give us lasting and stable love in his service.
*Hail Mary*

10 Sweet lady St Mary, for the joy and pity you felt when your sweet son commended you to his closest disciple, cousin and virgin, St John the Evangelist, and said 'Woman, behold your son', beseech him to have pity on us and grant us true and right compassion for our neighbours, and for his body which is holy church.
Amen
*Canticle. Nunc dimittis* [as in text **1**, canticle at compline]
*Our father*
*Hail Mary*

11 Sweet lady St Mary, for the joy you felt when truly with your virtuous eyes you saw your sweet son, our dear Lord Jesus Christ, living, whom you had seen die on the Cross; just as you truly believed he would rise again from death as he had promised his disciples, beseech him to give us true belief and firm faith. Amen
*Hail Mary*

12 Sweet lady St Mary, for the joy you felt when you saw with your blessed eyes your dear sweet son, our Lord Jesus Christ, ascend to heaven in the flesh he took from you, beseech him to let us live in such a way that we can firmly hope to attain the joy he promised to them [his apostles] and to us, his servants. Amen
*Hail Mary*

13 Sweet lady St Mary, for the joy you felt when the Holy Spirit descended into you and into those who loved our most sweet Lord, your son, on the day of Pentecost – he who enveloped you in love and illumined you with all truth – beseech him to give us true charity.
*Hail Mary*

14 Sweet lady St Mary, for the joy you felt in the glorious guidance of holy church, and in the miracles wrought by the apostles in the name of your sweet son while you remained in this world, and especially for the great longing you felt to attain the joy into which you had seen your son enter, beseech him to let us hate this life and despise this world, and give us hope and true desire to attain the joy he has promised to those who love him.
*Hail Mary*

15 Sweet lady St Mary, for the great joy you felt when your sweet son removed you from this exile and elevated you above all the angels in heaven, and placed you at his blessed right side, be our surety when we must go hence from this woeful prison, protect us from our enemy, and lead us to the glorious face of your sweet son, our Lord Jesus Christ.
Amen
[*Canticle*] *Benedictus dominus* [Luke 1, 68–79]
Blessed be the Lord [God of Israel: because he hath visited and wrought the redemption of his people:
And hath raised up an horn of salvation to us, in the house of David his servant.
As he spoke by the mouth of his holy prophets, who are from the beginning.
Salvation from our enemies, and from the hand of all that hate us.
To perform mercy to our Fathers; and to remember his holy testament.

The oath which he swore to Abraham our father; that he would grant to us,
That being delivered from the hand of our enemies, we may serve him without fear.
In holiness and justice before him, all our days.
And thou child, shalt be called the prophet of the Highest: for thou shalt go before the face of the Lord to prepare his ways.
To give knowledge of salvation to his people, unto the remission of their sins.
Through the bowels of the mercy of our God, in which the Orient, from on high, hath visited us.
To enlighten them that sit in darkness, and in the shadow of death: to direct our feet into the way of peace.
Glory be to the Father, and to the Son, and to the Holy Ghost.
As it was in the beginning, is now, and shall be, world without end. Amen]
[*Our father*]
*Hail Mary*

### 12.4 Eleanor Percy's *Gaude virgo mater Christi*

*Gawde, Vergine and mother beinge*

Arundel Hours

British Library MS Arundel 318, fol. 152r–152v

Middle English, except for Latin opening word *Gaude* 'rejoice' and Latin final line in each verse; the Latin words are integrated into the Middle English sentence structure

Refs: for Latin hymn, see Meersseman 1958–1960, vol. 2, 204; Wilmart 1932, 329 n. 1

Ed.: Barratt 1992, 279–281; other Middle English versions of the Latin hymn in Saupe 1998, 48–49; 176–77; 274–76

Eleanor Percy's prayer is an additional entry at the end of the manuscript. The prayer was added at the end of the fifteenth or beginning of the sixteenth century. The text is a sophisticated rendering, three-quarters in Middle English and one quarter in Latin, of one of the most popular Latin hymns to the Virgin. The integration of the Latin words into the Middle English sentence structure is smoothly and cleverly achieved. The Latin text is found in the supplementary contents of many books of hours. The Latin hymn occurs twice, for instance, in the De Mohun Hours, the second time with rich historiation of the capital letter at the beginning of each line (Boston Public Library MS 124, fols 31v–32r; 105v). The hymn invokes Mary's Five Joys – Annunciation + Conception, Nativity, Resurrection, Ascension, Assumption – and culminates in an appeal for help at the moment of death. The reference to Mary's conceiving through the ear in the opening verse is to be explained by the belief that the Word of God spoken by Gabriel at the Annunciation entered her body through her ear, and the Word of God was Christ. For a visual image of this manner of conception see the frontispiece to this volume (from Isabel Ruddok's Hours, Bristol Public Library MS 14, fol. 14v), where the child Christ is flying in towards Mary's ear in the upper left-hand part of the picture. Eleanor Percy is named by her sister Anne Arundel as the 'compiler' of the poem at the end of the text. Eleanor and Anne were daughters of Henry Percy, duke of Northumberland.

*Prayer of Eleanor Percy, duchess of Buckingham*

1 *Rejoice*, virgin and mother
Of Christ, both God and king,
Who conceived him with your blessed ear
*Through the messenger Gabriel.*

2 *Rejoice*, Virgin of all humility,
Showing us your son's humanity
When he was born of you without pain
*In lily-white purity.*

3 *Rejoice*, flower of your lord and son,
Who died without guilt for our redemption;
To your great joy and our salvation
*His Resurrection shines.*

4 *Rejoice*, for Christ has ascended
With all triumph to eternal bliss,
From which he first came down
*Of his own volition.*

5 *Rejoice*, sweet rose, at your blessed fortune;
Your assumption to the angels,
There to dwell evermore in joy,
*In the court of heaven.*

6 *Rejoice*, Virgin and mother of grace,
Pray to your son for our sins,
So that we come to that heavenly place
*In the company of the saints,*

7 Where the fruit of your womb, truly,
To our great comfort, dear lady,
Will reign everlastingly
*In perpetual joy.*

8 This prayer was compiled – God pardon her soul –
By the right noble duchess of Buckingham,

The late Eleanor Percy of virtuous memory
*Attested in truth.*

Say one *Our father*, one *Hail Mary* and one creed
For her soul and for all Christian souls

## 13 The Sorrows of the Virgin Mary

*[D]uce dame seinte Marie pur icele anguisse*
De Reydon Hours
CUL Dd.4.17, fols 76v–77v
Anglo-Norman
No ref. found in Dean and Boulton 2000
See note on additions to the manuscript, **6.1**

The Sorrows of the Virgin occur less frequently than the Joys in medieval English texts and images, although the sufferings of Christ are powerfully represented in prayers such as the Threefold Pity of Jesus, **8** (also from the De Reydon Hours), and the Fifteen Oes of St Bridget, **9.1**. The latter was very frequently included in books of hours from the early fifteenth century onwards. The present text is presented in five sections, which represent Five Sorrows in approximate chronological sequence; the third looks backward and forward over the whole of Jesus's life on earth. Section one focuses on the tale of Joseph finding Mary pregnant and wondering whether to leave her (Matthew 1:19); section two on the prophecy of Simeon that a sword will pierce her heart (Luke 3:34–35); section three on the flight into Egypt and also on the poverty and travail of the whole of Jesus's earthly life, and his mother's witnessing of it; section four on the Crucifixion; section five on Mary's longing to be with Christ in heaven, and her sorrow in witnessing the sufferings of the apostles and the early church. Each of the Sorrows is matched to a petition for help in a particular need: section one for anxiety, section two for fearfulness, section three for pain and travail, section four for sorrowfulness, section five for distress and longing to be with Mary. The rubric gives instructions for the Sorrows to be followed by Magnificat and 'Our father', which are therefore inserted in square brackets [] at the appropriate point; in fact the prayers are followed in the manuscript by the anthem *Salve regina*. The structure is in contrast to more formal and abstract sequences of Sorrows as found, for instance, in the Bridgettine compilations (not books of hours) British Library MS Harley 494, fols 101r–104r (Seven Sorrows), and Lambeth Palace Library MS 546, fols 7v–20v (Fifteen Sorrows), where Sorrows in chronological sequence are matched in complex penitential structures with compassion, contrition, and appeals for cleansing of senses, wits, and body.

*These five Sorrows are excerpted from the gospel for the servants of our lady. To be followed by* Magnificat. *Say the whole canticle right through to the end, with* Glory be to the father, *and then one* Our father

1 Sweet lady St Mary, for the anguish you felt when St Joseph your husband found you pregnant and requested you to leave secretly, comfort me and all those who serve you and are in anguish. Amen

2 Sweet lady St Mary, for the fear that you felt when Simeon told you the people would gainsay your son and he must suffer death, comfort me and all those who serve you and are fearful. Amen

3 Sweet lady St Mary, for the pain you suffered for seven years in your exile in Egypt and all your travail in following your beloved son in his life of poverty, from the hour when he was born of you so poor that you had nowhere to lay him except in the manger, to the time when he hung on the Cross before you and all his friends, comfort me and all those who suffer pain and travail. Amen

4 Sweet lady St Mary, for the sorrow you had when you saw his blood gush forth, his blessed body all pale and disfigured like a leper's, his arms and his hands pierced and swollen, and his eyes running with tears, and you heard at the same time the abusive reproaches and curses that the Jews and pagans and thieves spoke to him, and the words with which he commended you to St John, and his piteous cry when he lowered his head and gave up his spirit, at which the whole earth trembled and all creatures were struck with fear, and you saw his side pierced and his sinews severed, comfort me and all those who serve you and are sorrowful. Amen

5 Sweet lady St Mary, for the great longing you had to come to your most dear son, and the persecution that you saw in holy church when they took and beat the apostles, and killed and stoned the friends of your sweet son, comfort me and all those who serve you and who are in distress and desire to come to you.

6 Commend us, sweet lady, to the angel who watched over you, St Gabriel, and pray the Holy Spirit who comforted you in all your sufferings to comfort us. Amen

Magnificat [as in text **1**, canticle at vespers]
Our father
Hail Mary

*Anthem. Salve regina* [as in text **1** post-compline]

## 14 Prayers to Mary for help at the hour of death

**14.1** *O Maria piissima*
Malling Abbey Hours
Oxford, Bodleian Library MS Gough liturg. 9, fols 233v–234r
Latin rubric and verse prayer
Ref.: *RH* 13213; Ed. *AH*, Vol. 15, p. 140, no. 115

This prayer occurs as early as the twelfth century, for instance in the Winchester Psalter of Henry of Blois, and is found in many books of hours, and in other prayer books. In the De Mohun Hours, Boston Public Library MS 124, it is preceded by a rubric which was crossed out at or after the Reformation, presumably by Protestant objectors to the cult of Mary (fol. 119v). In the Madresfield Hours (Wormsley Court, Getty Library, fol. 95r), it was added on one of a number of pages which were originally left blank, probably for illustrations, and subsequently glued together.

*Whoever says this prayer daily will see the blessed Virgin Mary without doubt before death*

O most holy Mary,
Brightest star of the sea,
Mother of mercy,
And chamber of purity,

Pray for me to the lord
Jesus Christ your son,
That he deliver me from evil
And cause me to rejoice in all good things,

Release me from vices,
Give light from darkness,
Grant tranquillity
And keep me in peace;

And when the end of life comes,
Reveal yourself to my eyes,
So that through you I may escape
The terror of Satan,

That I may have you as my guide
In returning to my home,
Lest the fiery devil
Trouble my journey with envy,

Throwing up many things,
And false accusations,
Until the steward receives me,

The archangel Michael,

Whose task it is
To rescue all good people
From the devil
And restore them to paradise.
Amen

**14.2** *Deprecor te sancta Maria mater dei pietate plenissima*
Norwich Hours
Norwich Castle Museum MS 158.926/4f., fol. 157r
Latin prose

For the possibility that the 'sinful woman' suppliant was Katherine Bakon see notes to **17.1** above; see also **7.1**.

Saint Mary, most merciful mother of God, daughter of the supreme king, glorious mother, mother of orphans, consolation of the desolate, path for those who are lost, salvation for those who trust in you, virgin before giving birth, virgin in birth, virgin after birth, fountain of mercy, fountain of salvation and grace, fountain of charity and joy, consolation and indulgence, I pray you to intercede for me, a sinful woman, in the sight of your son, so that through his holy mercy and your holy intercession he may grant me before death and on my dying day pure confession and remission of sins, and life and peace everlasting to all the faithful, living and dead. Through Christ [our Lord. Amen]

## 15 Prayers in time of pestilence

**15.1** *Stella celi extirpavit*
De Mohun Hours
Boston Public Library MS 124, fol. 33r
Frequently found, with variations, in books of hours; e.g. Carew-Poyntz Hours, Cambridge, Fitzwilliam Museum MS 48, fol. 1v (with a different final prayer, or collect)
Latin verse
Ref.: *RH* 19438

Mary, the star of heaven and star of the sea, is seen as the cure for the mortal pestilence implanted by the fall – the original sin of Adam and Eve in the garden of Eden.

The star of heaven who suckled the Lord with her milk, rooted out
The mortal pestilence that the first parent of mankind implanted;
May that star now graciously constrain the constellations
Whose battles are delivering the people to the ulcer of dire death.
O glorious star of the sea, give us help and protection from the plague.
Hear us, for your son honours you, and denies you nothing;
Jesus, save us, as your virgin mother prays for us.

*Verse*
Pray for us, holy mother of God,
*Response*
So that we may be made worthy [of the promise of Christ]

[*Prayer*]
God of mercy, God of pity, God of forgiveness, you have taken pity on the affliction of your people, and have said to the avenging angel who is striking them down, 'It is enough, hold back your hand'; for love of that glorious star whose precious breasts you so gently sucked, countering the venom of our sins, grant us the help of your grace, so that we may be freed from pestilence and ill-prepared death, and saved from the assault of perdition.
God, you who live and reign, now and evermore. Amen

**15.2** *Sancte deus, sancte fortis, sancte et immortalis*
Brotherton Hours
Leeds University Library, Brotherton Collection MS 3, fols 1v–2r
English rubric, Latin prose text

There is an abbreviated version, with holy names in Greek as well as Latin, in Elizabeth Scrope's Hours, CUL Dd.6.1, fols 143r–v. The manuscripts were both written in the fifteenth century; and in both, these prayers are late-fifteenth-century additions – added presumably by owners to whom protection against the plague was an urgent necessity. Pope Sixtus, referred to in the rubric, is probably Sixtus IV (in office 1471–1484). The king is probably Edward IV (reigned 1461–1483). There was a renewed outbreak of the plague in the north of England in 1471, which would fit these dates.

A clear T-bar cross is drawn three times in the manuscript margin: beside 'This sign is over us'; 'Place this sign of salvation'; and 'May the God of Abraham.' The cross is represented in the translated text by **T**.

*This prayer was sent by Pope Sixtus to the king, to be said devoutly against the plague*

Holy God, holy mighty one, holy and immortal, Lamb of God who takes away the sins of the world, have pity on us.
**T** This sign is over us, the light of your face; Lord, you have given joy to my heart.

**T** Place this sign of salvation in the homes in which we live and do not let the avenging angel of heaven enter in. Place this sign, Lord, protect us, and the noxious pestilence will not be in us.
Have pity on me, Lord, have pity on us so that we may be delivered from this epidemic of the plague.
Let us pray:
Visit us, Lord, we pray, and protect our home from all snares of the enemy; keep them far away; and may your holy angels guard us, the inhabitants of this house, in peace, and bless us always; and may we be delivered from all pestilence, and from sudden and ill-prepared death. Through Christ our Lord. Amen
**T** May the God of Abraham, the God of Isaac, the God of Jacob be with us, for though we walk in the midst of the shadow of death we shall fear no evils because you are with us.
Our father
Hail Mary
Hear [our prayer]

### 16 Office of St Anne, and prayers to St Anne, mother of Mary

Although the narratives about her are entirely apocryphal, St Anne was one of the most important saints of the later Middle Ages, in the liturgy, in supplementary prayers in books of hours, and in visual images.

#### 16.1 Matins from the Office of St Anne

*Incipit matutine de sancta Anna matre Marie*
Percy Hours
British Library, MS Harley 1260, fols 79r–82v
Latin
Ref.: for *Golden Legend* narratives of St Anne, see Stace 1998

The Percy Hours are exceptional among lay people's books of hours in including not only *memoriae*, or commemorations, of St Anne, but also a full Office of St Anne for all the canonical hours, complete with psalms and readings. It has three readings at matins which recount the chief apocryphal medieval tales of Anne, as recorded in the thirteenth-century *Golden Legend* of James of Voragine. In the rubrics for this Office, the usual sequence of the headings 'Verse' + 'Response' is reversed, so the responses come first; at the very end there are two responses.

*Here begins matins of St Anne, mother of Mary*
Lord, open my lips
And my mouth will speak your praise.
Lord, [make haste to] help [me]

*Invitatory. Adoremus Christum regem*
Let us adore Christ the king whom Mary bore,
Whose mother St Anne shone in glory with her child.

*Psalm 94 (95) Venite* [*exultemus*]
Come, let us [praise the Lord with joy, let us joyfully sing to God, our saviour: let us come before his presence with thanksgiving, and make a joyful noise to him with psalms.
For the Lord is a great God, and a great King above all gods: for the Lord will not reject his people: for in his hand are all the ends of the earth: and he indeed observes the heights of the mountains.
For the sea is his, and he made it, and his hands established the dry land: come, let us adore, and fall down before God: let us weep in the presence of the Lord, who made us, for he indeed is the Lord our God; moreover we are his people, and the sheep of his pasture.
Today, if you shall hear his voice, harden not your hearts, as in the affliction according to the day of temptation in the wilderness: where your fathers tempted me, they proved me, and saw my works.
Forty years was I nigh unto this generation, and I said: These always err in heart; these men indeed have not known my ways: to whom I swore in my wrath: They shall not enter into my rest.
Glory be to the father, and to the son, and to the Holy Ghost. As it was in the beginning, is now, and ever shall be, world without end. Amen]

*Hymn. Gaudet chorus fidelium*
The chorus of the faithful rejoices, the company of believers sings
Of Anne, blessed woman, Anne, peerless mother,
From whom came forth Mary, who alone gave birth unsullied;
Save [us], key of purity, bringing forth your son the ruler;
Both your noble parents, both to be commended,
Shining lamps of the world, gleaming with divine light;
Glory be to the trinity, praise, power and grace,
Glory, honour and might for ever, world without end. Amen

*Anthem. Sol eternus*
The eternal sun chose Anne of old
So that she should bear his mother in the flesh.

*Response*
Blessed progeny, of whom Christ was born;
*Verse*
O how glorious is the one who bore the king of heaven.

[*Prayer*]
Our father

*Jube domine benedicere*
Let us be blessed, O Lord.

May the son of the virgin grant us chastity in mind and body. Amen
*First reading. Anna vero sic lamentante*
Behold, while Anne lamented in this manner the angel of the lord appeared to her saying, 'Anne, Anne, God has heard your voice and your prayer. Behold, you will conceive and bear a child and word of your seed will spread to all the world.' At this Anne was comforted and joyful, and answered saying, 'For this, whatsoever child I shall bring forth, whether male or female, I shall offer to my lord, and it will serve [the lord] all the days of its life.'
Lord, have mercy on us, thanks be to God.

*Response*
Let us celebrate this day with joy, on which blessed mother Anne ascended to heaven;
*Verse*
From whom came forth the virgin and mother of life.

*Jube domine benedicere*
Let us be blessed, O Lord.
May the mother and virgin defend us from the malignant enemy. Amen

*Second reading. Itaque consurgens ascende*
'So arise and go up to Jerusalem. And when you reach the gate which is called golden because it is gilded, there, as a miraculous sign, go to meet your husband for whose safety you are troubled.' After which, behold, two stood beside her clothed in white garments, saying, 'Happy Anne. Behold, Joachim is coming with his shepherds.'

*Tu autem domine*
[Have mercy on us] O Lord

*Response. In redempcionis nostre*
In the work of our redemption and salvation
Blessed Anne appears like the root of the tree,
*Verse. Ex qua virga trahit*
From which the twig brought forth the fount of life, bearing the almond, Anne

*Jube domine*
Let us be blessed, O Lord.
May holy mother Anne help us in every tribulation and distress. Amen

*Third reading. Angelus enim domini descendit*
The angel of the lord descended and said to him, 'The lord has heard your prayer. Rise up and offer a sacrifice. For behold, your wife Anne will conceive and bear a child.' Therefore Joachim called his shepherds, saying, 'Bring me ten unblemished yearling sheep which will be for my lord; and bring twelve young deer-calves which will be for the priests;

and I will sacrifice one hundred sheep which will be for all the people to share.'
Lord, bless [your people]

*Response. Bethleem natale solum*
Bethlehem, the native soil of mother Anne, is cherished,
Home of the eternal and celestial bread,
*Verse. Que super nos pascit*
Which feeds, beyond ourselves, dwellers in all lands,
Home [of the eternal and celestial bread].

Glory to the father [and to the son, and to the Holy Spirit].
Home [of the eternal and celestial bread].

[Ambrosian hymn]. *Te deum* [*laudamus*]
We praise thee, O God, [we acknowledge thee to be the Lord.
All the earth doth worship thee, the father everlasting.
To thee all angels cry aloud, the heavens and all the powers therein.
To thee Cherubim and Seraphim continually do cry:
Holy, holy, holy, Lord God of Sabaoth;
Heaven and earth are full of the majesty of thy glory.
The glorious choir of the Apostles praise thee,
The admirable company of the Prophets praise thee,
The white-robed army of Martyrs praise thee.
The holy Church throughout all the world doth acknowledge thee,
The Father of an infinite majesty;
Thine honourable, true and only son;
Also the Holy Ghost, the Comforter.
Thou art the King of glory, O Christ,
Thou art the everlasting Son of the Father.
When thou tookest upon thee to deliver man, thou didst not abhor the Virgin's womb.
When thou hadst overcome the sting of death, thou didst open the kingdom of heaven to all believers.
Thou sittest at the right hand of God, in the glory of the Father.
We believe that thou shalt come to be our Judge.
We pray thee, therefore, help thy servants, whom thou hast redeemed with thy precious blood.
Make them to be numbered among thy Saints, in glory everlasting.
O Lord, save thy people and bless thine inheritance.
Govern them, and lift them up for ever.
Day by day we magnify thee;
And we praise thy name for ever, yea, for ever and ever.
Vouchsafe, O Lord, this day to keep us without sin.
O Lord, have mercy upon us, have mercy upon us.
O Lord, let thy mercy be showed upon us, as we have hoped in thee.
O Lord, in thee have I hoped: let me not be confounded for ever.]

*Response. Celeste beneficium*
The celestial miracle entered St Anne,
*Response. Per quam nobis nata est*
From whom was born for us the virgin Mary.

## 16.2 Invocation of St Anne within the Little Office at lauds

*Celeste beneficium introivit*

Amesbury Hours

Cambridge University Library MS Ee.6.16, fol 31r

Latin prose

This invocation occurs in this manuscripst among prayers to numerous saints in lauds of the Little Office; appeals to the saints were often appended at this point. For further commemorations added to this manuscript, see **16.3**.

*Celeste beneficium introivit*
The celestial boon entered into Anne, through whom the Virgin Mary was born for us.
\Abundance and riches will be in the house, and righteousness will remain for ever and ever/.
The lord will gaze favourably upon her. God will not be moved to anger around her.

*Deus qui beate Anne tantam graciam*
God who deigned to bestow on blessed Anne such grace that she was worthy to bear the most blessed Mary, your mother, in her glorious womb, grant us through the intercession of mother and daughter the plenitude of your mercy, so that through the prayers of those women whose memory we enfold in pious love, we may deserve to attain the heavenly Jerusalem.
Through Jesus Christ our Lord.

## 16.3 Four commemorations of St Anne

Amesbury Hours

Cambridge University Library MS Ee.6.16, fols 9r–10v

Latin anthems or hymns, verse + response, prayer

These four commemorations are in material added at the beginning of the manuscript, which suggests that they were of great importance to an early owner. The second is for use on St Anne's day, 26 July. Similar prayers to St Anne are found in the Beaufort Hours and the Queen Mary Hours (British Library MSS Royal 2.A.18 and Sloane 2565). The final item, the anthem *Gaude felix Anna* + verse + collect *Domine Jhesu Christe qui beate*

*Anne tantam graciam donare dignatus es*, occurs also in Elizabeth Scrope's Hours, CUL Dd.6.1, fols 22r–v, preceded in that manuscript by an illumination on fol. 21v of St Anne with a book on her lap, and Mary with baby reaching out towards the book (see plate 3).

**16.3.1**

*Hymn. Anna parens sublimis domine*
Anne parent of the sublime lady,
We praise you, mother of mercy,
Shining gem of the court of heaven,
For love of your daughter.

*Verse*
Pray for us, blessed Anne,
So that we may be worthy of the eternal promise.

*Prayer. Deus qui beatam Annam diu sterilem*
God who chose to make fruitful blessed Anne, barren for so long, with a glorious child who brought salvation for humankind, grant that all who venerate the mother for love of the daughter may deserve to rejoice in the presence of both at the hour of death.
Through Christ our [Lord]

**16.3.2**

*Anthem. Ad felicis Anne festum*
All people throng to the festival of happy Anne,
Whose child has driven away the dark night of the world;
Through Mary, star of the sea,
Bride of heaven,
And through Christ her son –
Eternal death perishes in him.

*Prayer*
May mother and daughter be our support,
Like those laying roses and lilies as the bridegroom arises.
Pray for us, blessed Anne, so that we may be made worthy [of the eternal promise].

*Prayer*
Almighty everlasting God, graciously keep from us all adversities of the world, so that through the intercession of St Anne, mother of blessed Mary, mother of your son, you will remove all evils and grant us all promises. Through our Lord Jesus Christ.

3. St Anne and the Education of the Virgin. Elizabeth Scrope's Hours. Cambridge University Library MS Dd.6.1, fol. 21v, original size of picture 18 x 12 cm

**16.3.3**

*Hymn. Anna sancta Jhesu Christi*
Blessed Anne, you brought forth
The mother of Jesus Christ;
You conceived the mother of God,
Remedy for sinners,
And having conceived her you bore
The refuge for the fallen.
Hail, temple of God's temple,
Temple of peace for us,
Temple of the primal light.
Hail, root of true hope,
Take pity on my spirit;
Light of eternal light,
You can implore from him
Whatever you will, to be granted to us
Through your holy daughter;
Let us reign with you,
And contemplate with you
The glory of the celestial temple.
St Anne, gain for us
The joys which are yours
In eternal glory. Amen

*Prayer. Deus qui sanctam Annam*
God who provided St Anne as temple of blessed Mary the Virgin, and who chose her as parent of your own mother, with virgin womb, may we through her merits build your temple in this present world, and, in the world to come, attain the glory of the celestial temple.

**16.3.4**

*Anthem. Gaude felix Anna que concepisti prolem*
Rejoice, fruitful Anne, who conceived the child
Who was to give birth to the saviour of the world;
Rejoice, fruitful Anne, mother of the great child;
From you went forth the glittering star of the sun on high.
Rejoice, fruitful Anne, mother of Mary,
Virgin who bore God, and is mother of the Messiah.
Rejoice, fruitful Anne; you alone were worthy
To be mother of Jesus Christ's virgin mother.
Rejoice, fruitful Anne, rejoice without end;
Offer prayers for me to the queen of heaven.

*Verse*
May mother and daughter pray for me,

[*Response*]
Whispering to him like incense and lilies.

*Prayer*
God who raised up blessed Anne, excellent mother of your sweet mother, to the joys of celestial life, let us, we pray, through her glorious merits attain eternal bliss; through whose salvation-bringing progeny you deigned to take our human flesh, Jesus Christ, our Lord and your son, who lives and reigns with you in the fellowship of the Holy Spirit, God eternal, world without end. Amen

### 16.4 Anglo-Norman salutations to St Anne

*Ave duz comencement*

Amesbury Hours

Cambridge University Library MS Ee.6.16, fols 10r–10v

Also in British Library, MS Egerton 2781, fols 41v–43r

Anglo-Norman French

Ref.: Dean and Boulton 2000, no. 920

Like the preceding Latin items, the Anglo-Norman text is part of extra material added at the beginning of this manuscript. The reference to Mary as born of the line of kings and a queen, in verse 2, is puzzling. Biblical genealogies usually trace the line only through the fathers. Of course, a king, such as David or his son Solomon (both of whom occur in Christ's genealogy as traced in Matthew 1, 1–17), may be assumed in medieval terms to have had a queen. Perhaps the writer had in mind the Queen of Sheba, who visited Solomon (1 Kings 10; 2 Chronicles 9). The genealogy of Matthew goes back through Joseph (husband of Mary, but not Christ's father), rather than through Mary. The explanation usually given for this difficulty is that Joseph and Mary must have been cousins, and therefore shared the same ancestry, from a few generations back.

The fifth and last verse of **16.4** is addressed to Mary, rather than Anne. It seems most likely that the fourth verse also, where the theme of 'noble lineage' is taken up again, is addressed to Mary.

1 Hail glorious St Anne,
Sweet commencement
Of joy without end,
Of the mother of God and bride,
Who by giving birth –
Source of great joy to her –
Saved us from death and destruction
And from hideous pain.

2 Hail to you, whose progeny
Was born of the root

Of Jesse, David and Solomon,
Of kings and a queen;
You, who for our redemption
Bore in your womb
The one who, uncorrupted,
Gave birth as a virgin.

3 Hail – for barrenness
You long suffered shame,
Yet with holy meekness
You fulfilled your daily tasks.
I ask that your offspring –
For her it is no burden –
May grant me chastity
And cleanse me of all evil.

4 Hail, my joy and my refuge,
Lady of noble lineage,
Full of grace and virtue;
Guide my travels,
Be my aid and my shield
On this pilgrimage,
And may God through his great goodness
Grant us to sojourn with him.

5 Hail my lady, in whom I trust,
So gentle, good, and holy;
With all my heart I cry for mercy,
You have all my devotion;
Carry my request
To the one who was born of you,
That he may save my soul from the enemy
And my body from shame.

## 17 Latin prayers to further saints

### 17.1 St Katherine

*Oreisun de seinte Katerine: seinte pucele Katerine*

Norwich Hours

Norwich Castle Museum MS 158.926/4f., fols 154r–v

Anglo-Norman prose

Refs: Dean and Boulton 2000, no. 929; Legge 1963, 66–72; Wogan-Browne 1996, 67–68

The manuscript has an obit of Katerine Bakon dated 1377, several decades after it was originally made (see 'Manuscript sources of translated texts' above). If she was the original owner of the manuscript, as is entirely possible, this may have prompted the inclusion of the prayer to St Katherine, her name-saint, in her book. However, the inclusion of a prayer to this famous saint does not depend on prompting of this kind.

St Katherine had special importance for literate women. It was said that she successfully defended Christianity in debate with the pagan masters of Alexandria. An Anglo-Norman life of the saint, not contained in a book of hours, was written by a nun.

1 Holy maid Katherine, I pray to you by the honour which God accorded you that day when you vanquished the learned masters and then performed miracles regarding those who were thrown in the fire, for you saved them that day from animosity and wrath and rancour through your blessed humility; dear maid, by that great honour which God showed to you in prison when he visited you himself and brought joy and solace, help me to come to Jesus, who has all power to alleviate my sorrows and bring me to joy.

2 Maid Katherine, for the honour which God granted you the day you saw the wheel set up before you, to cut you to cruel death, and God sent you his angel and cut the wheel into pieces – by that honour help me every day to come to Jesus my saviour, that I may serve him faithfully.

3 Dear maid Katherine, you rejoiced when your head was cut off by the evil people who hated you; you remained all white rather than covered in blood, thanks be to God, which signifies incontrovertibly that you were a pure virgin, and the angels of God lifted up your body and carried it with great joy to Mount Sinai, laid it there in its bed and took your soul with them and presented it to God.

4 Dear maid, by the honour granted you now for your travail, pray for me to Jesus, the son of Mary, that by his holy pity he may preserve me from mortal sin, from evil and misadventure, and from everlasting hell, and keep me today and every day from speaking evil and thinking evil, from evil death and disaster.

### 17.2 St Margaret

*Gaude virgo Margareta*

Brotherton Hours

Leeds University Library, Brotherton Collection MS 3, fols 51r–52r

Latin verse and prose

Ref.: Legge 1963, 258

Ed.: *AH* 29, 112; with variations, from other manuscripts, mostly of English origin

The commemoration of St Margaret follows the usual pattern of anthem to the saint, followed by prose verse and response, and prayer to God. It is preceded by a full-page miniature of the saint rising from the belly of the dragon. Through tales of her miraculous delivery from the dragon's belly St Margaret became associated with safe passage in childbirth; she is the patron saint of women in labour, and copies of the Anglo-Norman *Life of St Margaret* were even placed on the breast of women in childbirth to act as a charm.

*Anthem*

1 Rejoice, virgin Margaret,
Who happily drove to pasture
Your foster-mother's flock;

2 Rejoice, scorning worldly pomp,
Champion martyr strong in faith,
Blossoming in modesty;

3 Rejoice, thrown into prison,
Trusting in the power of the Cross,
Triumphant over the monster;

4 Rejoice, virgin flagellated,
Comforted by the dove,
Spurning the assaults of the duke;

5 Rejoice in the prayer you gladly uttered
As you were beheaded for Christ,
Singing the greatest joys;

6 Rejoice, virgin, now in bliss,
So that a sound pleasing to our God
May be rendered in heaven.

*Verse*
Pray for us, blessed Margaret,
*[Response]*
So that we may be made worthy of the promise of Christ.

*Prayer*
Graciously listen to our prayer, we beseech you, Lord; mercifully hear our entreaties and bestow your mercy on us; and, in whatever necessity we may cry to you, may we obtain the gracious mercies of your consolation through the intercession of the blessed virgin Margaret. Amen

### 17.3 St Mary Magdalen

*Memoria de sancta Maria Magdalena: Gaude pia Magdalena*
Queen Mary Hours
British Library MS Sloane 2565, fols 24r–24v
Latin verse and prose

There was no doubting that Mary Magdalen's place in Christian history was of paramount importance. Her story, conflated with those of other New Testament women called Mary, gave hope to the penitent that they might win Christ's love. The reference to the one cast forth from the cave would accord more with the early Christian legend of St Mary of Egypt, a penitent harlot who went to live in the desert.

*Anthem. Gaude pia Magdalena*

Rejoice, pious Magdalen, hope of salvation, vessel of life, assurance of the fallen;
Rejoice, gentle advocate of the penitent, model granted to the wretched after their vices;
Rejoice, blessed and pleasing to God, whose sins were dismissed by special grace;
Rejoice, you who washed Christ's feet, earning such great tokens of love;
Rejoice, you who were first worthy to enjoy the sight of your redeemer resurrected in glory,
Rejoice, you who at each of the seven hours were cast forth from the cave to the paths of heaven;
Rejoice, you who are now elevated and set in glory with Christ in the celestial court.
Make us penitent here, so that after death we may be allotted the joys of true light. Amen

*Verse*
Pray for us, blessed Mary Magdalen,
[*Response*]
So that we may become worthy of the promise of Christ.

*Prayer*
God, who made the penitence of blessed Mary Magdalen so pleasing and agreeable to you that you not only forgave her sins, but also truly brought light to her frailty through the cordial grace of your love of her, grant us, we pray, to weep deservedly for the sins we have committed, so that we, too, may be worthy of holy indulgence, and may experience the clemency of your grace in response to all our petitions. Through Christ our Lord. Amen

### 17.4 SS Katherine, Margaret and Mary Magdalen

*Katerina Margareta virgines sanctissime*
Syon Abbey Hours
Syon Abbey MS 2, fols 207r–207v
Latin verse and prose

This *memoria*, or commemoration, of the saints is unusual in combining the New Testament saint, Mary Magdalen, with the early Christian virgin martyrs, Katherine of Alexdandria and Margaret of Antioch. For prayers to each of these saints alone, see the preceding texts.

*[Anthem]*

Katherine and Margaret, most holy virgins,
Magdalen pleasing to God,
Join in prayer to Christ,
So that he may deign to keep us chaste in body
And bring us cleansed of sins to the court of heaven.

*Verse*
Pray for us, all the elect of Christ
*Response*
So that we may become worthy of celestial grace.

*Let us pray*
God who caused your most holy virgins Katherine and Margaret to reach heaven through the martyr's palm, and granted most blessed Mary Magdalen pardon for all her sins, graciously grant that through their intercessory prayers and merits and radiant chastity we may deserve to be honoured and absolved from the fetters of sin. Through Jesus Christ our Lord.

### 17.5 St Ursula

*O beata Ursula deo predilecta*
Syon Abbey Hours
Syon Abbey MS 2, fols 206r–206v
Latin anthem + verse and response + prose prayer to God

The legend of the early Christian virgin martyr St Ursula was very popular in the Middle Ages. Said to have been the daughter of a king of Britain, she was especially honoured at Cologne, where she and her 11,000 virgin companions were allegedly killed on their journey home from a pilgrimage to Rome, as a consequence of rejecting the advances of would-be suitors.

*Anthem*

1 O blessed Ursula, beloved of God,
Reputed to descend from royal stock,
You were martyred for Christ's name;
I pray that you may protect my soul.

2 Your holy chastity coupled to you
Bishops and virgins whom God chose;
But the tyrant's ferocity martyred them,
To whom Christ gave a place with him in glory.

3 For this I pray, Ursula and your company,
Bring me solace at my death;
Be so strong against all my enemies
That through you heaven's gates are opened to me.

4 And you, holy virgins, blessed martyrs,
Given to cruel death with St Ursula,
Support not guilt but chastity;
Visit me at the point of death.

5 I pray, too, that I may feel through your prayer
Christ's abundant grace, flowing to me from him,
So that I may worthily be cleansed from filth of sin
And deserve to be saved from everlasting death.

*Verse*
Chosen virgins of God, pray for us,
*Response*
So that we may deserve to receive forgiveness of sins.

*Prayer*
God, who desired the most holy virgins Ursula and her companions, your martyrs, to suffer through constancy of chastity, graciously grant that through their merits and intercessions we may be preserved in chastity of body, and deserve to achieve the abundant grace through which our petitions will be heard. Through Christ our Lord.

## 17.6 St Zita

*Ave sancta famula Citha Jhesu Christi*

Syon Abbey Hours

Syon Abbey, Syon Abbey MS 2, fols 206v–207r

Latin anthem + verse and response + prose prayer to God

St Zita was the patron saint of those who served in households, and regarded as especially helpful in finding lost things. She was also 'specially invoked in places where there were perils from water or from dangerous bridges from one of which she was blown into the river and marvellously recovered' (*St. Paul's Eccl. Soc. Trans.* 3, 245). Perhaps especially suitable for Syon Abbey, for some of whose members the journey to and from Vadstena in Sweden, via the North Sea and Lynn in Norfolk, was a perilous necessity.

Her importance not only to the Bridgettine compiler of this prayer in the Syon Abbey Hours, but also to the original patron of the Bolton Hours, is indicated by the fact that the latter manuscript includes a miniature of the saint with donor portrait (fol. 40v).

*[Anthem]*

Hail Zita, holy servant of Jesus Christ.
Gratifying God's will with all your heart,
You fed the feeble and needy,
You helped the blind and the mute, the weak and the lame,
You sought always to give alms;
As virgin you delighted God and the church,
You hated deceit and iniquity entirely;
Prepare for us, too, the joy that you have earned.

*Verse*
Pray for us blessed Zita,
*Response*
So that we may be cleansed of all evils in this life.

*Let us pray*
God who adorned blessed Zita your servant in her lifetime with many miracles, grant, we beseech you, that all who ask her help for love of you, may through her deserts feel what is fitting for them. Through Jesus Christ our Lord.

## 17.7 St Susannah

DuBois Hours

Pierpont Morgan Library MS M.700, fols 29v–30v

Latin

Refs: Donovan 1991, 24; Hunt 1990, 82 *passim* for 'Susannah charms' used in healing; Miskimin 1969, for an elegant and popular Middle English stanzaic version of Susannah's tale, which, like this commemoration, dwells on human aspects of the Old Testament story, and delights in the natural and scriptural imagery of the garden.

This sequence of prayers, like one of the commemorations of St Anne in the Amesbury Hours, is inserted in a series of commemorations of the saints appended to lauds in the Little Office.

The Old Testament heroine Susannah is invoked as true and chaste wife, and also as the 'type' of the unjustly accused innocent. The anthem preceding the first prayer to God in this commemoration sets Susannah amidst the Old Testament imagery, especially of the Song of Songs, often associated with Mary, but transferred also to other notable heroines. Comparable versions of the concluding prayer, citing the miraculous saving of Susannah and others, are found in the De Reydon Hours (**6.3**), the Beatrice Hours (**20.1**), and in Isabel Ruddok's prayer (**21**). Susannah's help is sought especially in protecting women against slander, malicious gossip and backbiting. In the De Reydon Hours, an extra request for protection against backbiting and slander has been marked for insertion in the prayer (**6.3**).

*Of St Susannah*

*Anthem. Veni in ortum meum*

Come into my garden, my sister, my bride,
Put fruits in my bowl with my fragrances.

*Verse*
God chose her, pre-ordained before the dawn of time
*Reponse*
He makes her dwell in his tabernacle

*Prayer. Deus qui liberasti Susannam*
Almighty everlasting God who freed Susannah from false accusation and saved Jonah from the lions' den, and the three youths from the fiery furnace, and stretched out your hand to Peter in peril on the sea, now through the intercession of blessed Susannah and those whose names are called to mind, deign to free your servant Hawisia from all tribulations and troubles and slanders and snares of the fiend, and from the power of all enemies and those associated with them, because I do not know where else to turn except to you, O God. Through [Jesus] Christ [our Lord].

### 17.8 St Apollonia

*Hec est virgo sapiens*
Bolton Hours
York Minster Library Additional MS 2, fols 198v–199r
Latin

Apollonia is commended in this text as one of the wise virgins, who had trimmed their lamps and procured oil for them in anticipation of the coming of the lord (Matthew 25, 1–13). Another prayer to her is found in the Percy Hours, British Library MS Harley 1260. She was the patron saint of those suffering from toothache. In hagiographical accounts she was said to have been an aged deaconess, martyred in Alexandria in A.D. 249, during the general persecution of Christians; before her death all her teeth were knocked out. See Lesson ix for 9 February (when not in Lent) in the *Roman Breviary*:

> Apollonia, a virgin of Alexandria in the reign of the emperor Decius, when she was far advanced in years, was brought to the idols that she might worship them; despising them, she declared that worship ought only to be given to Jesus Christ, the true God. Whereupon all her teeth were broken and pulled out; then lighting a funeral pile, the impious torturers threatened to burn her alive, unless she would abjure Christ and adore the gods. She replied that she would suffer any kind of death for the faith of Jesus Christ. Upon this, they seized her, intending to burn her, when she stood for a moment, as though hesitating what the should do; then, escaping from their hold, she suddenly threw herself into the fire, for there burned within her the stronger fire of the Holy Ghost. Her body was soon consumed, and her most pure soul took flight to heaven, to the everlasting crown of martyrdom

*[Commemoration] of the virgin Apollonia*

*Anthem*

This is the wise virgin whom the lord found vigilant;
For your lovely face and beauty, listen, prosper, go forth and reign.

[*Prayer*]
God, for the honour of whose most holy name the blessed martyr and virgin Apollonia suffered the bitter knocking out of her teeth, be with us, we pray, so that we who commemorate her may be freed from toothache through her intercession. Through [Jesus Christ our Lord].

### 17.9 St Christopher

Christopher is best known today as the gentle giant who carried the Christ child on his shoulders across the river; he was also one of the early Christian martyrs. Christopher's help is attested in the legend of his appeal to Christ at the moment of death as cited in the prayers – that wherever an image of him was erected or prayers to him were uttered, help might be granted to those in need. He is invoked in books of hours in pleas for protection against many sources of suffering, and especially against the ravages of the plague, which afflicted people in England as in the rest of the Europe from the time of the first terrible epidemic, the Black Death of 1349. Prayers to St Christopher often occur in close proximity to prayers to

St Anne; this is the case both in the Beaufort Hours and the Queen Mary Hours. Both saints were regarded as very helpful in daily life.

### 17.9.1 Beaufort Hours

*Concede nobis quesumus*
Beaufort Hours
British Library, MS Royal 2.A.18, fol. 25r
Latin

*[Prayer]*
Grant, almighty and merciful God, that we who commemorate your martyr, blessed Christopher, through his holy merits and intercession may be saved from sudden and everlasting death, and from plague, famine, sickness, fear and sorrow, and all the wiles of all enemies; through you, Jesus Christ, whom he was worthy to carry [across the water]. Who live and reign ever world without end.

*Another prayer of St Christopher: Domine Jhesu Christe*
Lord Jesus Christ, who mercifully granted to your blessed martyr Christopher in answer to his prayer at the hour of his martyrdom, that in whatever place an image of him was placed or a prayer in memory of him was uttered, there should be no ingress of wrath or famine or fire or conflagration or sickness or plague or destruction of the people, keep me and defend me, your servant .N. and all my relations and the family gathered together in this house and all Christians. Who live and reign with [God the father, world without end].

*Another prayer. Presta quesumus*
Grant, we beseech you, almighty God that we who celebrate the memory of your blessed martyr, Christopher, through his merits and intercession may be saved from sudden and everlasting death. Through Jesus Christ our Lord. Amen

### 17.9.2 Queen Mary Hours

*Memoria de sancto Christofore martire*
British Library MS Sloane 2565, fols 20r–20vv
Latin anthem + prose

*Commemoration of St Christopher, martyr*
*[Anthem]. O sancte Christofore martir Jhesu Christi*

O holy Christopher, martyr of Jesus Christ,
Who suffered pain for Christ's name,
Give help to the wretched and to the sad world –
You, who have earned the kingdom of celestial light.
Whoever gazes on the image of saint Christopher,

Indeed on that day shall be seized by no illness;
Martyr Christopher, for the honour of the saviour
Make our minds worthy of the love of God;
Through the promise of Christ you have obtained what you asked,
Give the sorrowful people what you asked for at death;
Grant comfort and lift the burden from their mind,
Make the scrutiny of judgement less harsh for all people. Amen

*Verse*
Lord, you have crowned him with honour and glory, and have set him above the works of your hand.

*Prayer*
Grant, we beseech you, almighty and merciful God, that we who commemorate your blessed martyr, Christopher, may through his holy merits and intercession be freed from everlasting death and from sudden pestilence, famine, dread, and poverty, and from all the wiles of our enemies, through you, Jesus Christ, saviour of the world, whom he was worthy to carry on his shoulders. Who [live and reign] with God the father in the unity of the Holy Spirit, [one] God, world without end. Amen

### 17.9.3 Isabel Ruddok's Hours

*Tu Jhesus es testis*

Bristol Public Library MS 14, fol. 12r

Latin *memoria* anthem + prose prayer to God

On fol. 11v, facing the prayer, there is a whole-page miniature of St Christopher

Ref.: *RH* 34108

*[Anthem]*

Jesus, you are witness that wherever Christopher is named,
Snow, famine, plague, evil death will not prevail there,
Nor will mankind or animals suffer any kind of harm;
As the voice of Christ promptly conceded at the hour of Christopher's death.

Saint Christopher, martyr, for the honour of the saviour
Make our minds worthy through the love of God,
Through the promise of Christ, granted in answer to your petition.
Give the mournful people the boons you requested at the hour of death,
Grant solace and take away heaviness of mind;
May the last judgement yield life for all. Amen

*[Verse]*
Pray for us, blessed Christopher,

*[Response]*
So that we may be made worthy of the promise of Christ.

*[Prayer]*
Grant, we beseech you, almighty God, that we who commemorate your blessed martyr Christopher may be saved through his merits and intercession from plague, hunger, danger, fear, sorrow, and all perils of our enemies. Through our Lord Jesus Christ your son, who lives and reigns with you, one God without end. Amen

## 18 Latin prayers to the Guardian Angel

Prayers to the Guardian Angel are freqent in English books of hours. One of the most popular ones, *Ave gaude dulcissime mi angele qui es custos corporis mei* 'Hail, rejoice, sweetest angel, who are guardian of my body', is thought by Wilmart to be a fifteenth-century development of a twelfth-century prayer attributed to Reginald monk of St Augustine's Benedictine abbey, Canterbury (Wilmart 1932, 551–55). It occurs in additional material in the fourteenth-century De Mohun Hours, Boston Public Library 124, fols 108v–109r (not included in the present collection). The striking donor portrait attached to this prayer in the Beaufort Hours attests the power attributed to the Guardian Angel as protector against evil.

**18.1** *Angele qui meus es custos*
Beaufort Hours
British Library, MS Royal 2.A.18, fol. 26r
Latin verse

A donor portrait with angel accompanies these prayers. The donor holds a scroll inscribed *sub umbra alarum tuarum* 'beneath the protection of your wings'; the angel holds a scroll inscribed *dominus custodiat te ab omni malo* 'may the lord protect you from all evil'.

*Prayer. Angele qui meus es custos*
Angel, you who are my guardian, save, protect and guide me,
Entrusted to you by mercy from above.
Turn my mind from sin and the ancient fall,
Be a watchful companion to me, and lamp of life.
Faithful angel, wise companion, revered, benign,
Let me not be perturbed by fear of malignant death,
Lying in wait for me, though I deserve pain and hell.
Help me, I pray, not to fall into infernal fire,

*Response*
You to whose especial care I am entrusted.

*Prayer*

O holy and blessed angel of God, divine goodness entrusted me as a child through the sacrament of baptism to you, for you to watch over me and protect me; I beseech you by the one who assigned to you this task, guard and protect me from all wiles and contamination of malignant spirits hostile to me, who seek to bear away my soul. You, indeed, they respect and fear, because you are the good spirit of God, from whom you have received power over them. Through Christ our Lord.

**18.2** *Sancte angele dei*

Bolton Hours

York Minster Additional MS 2, fol. 199v

Latin prose

*Prayer to the Guardian Angel*

Holy angel of God, minister of the celestial empire, to whom almighty God has assigned guardianship of me; by his majesty and power I implore you, protect my soul and my senses from evil and perverse desires, and from gross thoughts, and from the delusions of malignant spirits; and my body from any bad and impure deed; and confirm me in just and holy works. After this life, lead my soul to eternal joy, where it may rejoice with God and his saints. Amen

## 19 Anglo-Norman prayer for safety in childbirth, attributed to Thomas Becket's mother

*Dampne dieu roy omnipotent*

Percy Hours

British Library MS Harley 1260, fols 176v–178v

Also in the DuBois Hours, Pierpont Morgan Library MS M.700, fols 141v–144v, without attribution to Thomas Becket's mother

Anglo-Norman verse

Ref.: Dean and Boulton 2000, no. 871

In the first long section of the text, addressing Jesus as king and incarnate man, the prayer rehearses his conception, gestation, birth, circumcision, presentation in the temple, and lactation. Then it appeals to him as father, for safety in childbirth, and also for the safety and wellbeing of the child to be born; the woman asks to be able to take it to church, and to achieve her own purification – the 'churching' rite by which women were declared cleansed and purified after giving birth (as in the Purification of Mary celebrated on 2 February, coinciding in the church calendar with the Presentation of Christ, as also with the pre-Christian festival of Candlemas). In the second section, the woman appeals to Mary, invoking the annunciation and conception, and the love of Christ, dwelling again on the lactation. Then she turns, as in the litany of saints, to the apostles, confessors, martyrs, holy virgins, and all saints. Finally she begs them all to appeal to Jesus on her behalf, and for her child. Throughout the prayer one senses the powerful interweaving of body and spirit, felt so keenly in parturition and the preparation for it, and intensified by the fear of death. The woman's requests for herself and for her child are both physical and spiritual: towards the end of the first section she wishes to bring the child to church and for it to receive the blessing of holy law, while at the same time she prays that it may 'never suffer loss of vital limb'; at the end, she begs that the child may arrive safely, and stay with her and her family in this world, and escape the clutches of the devil. Jesus is the physician of all ills, physical and spiritual.

*This prayer was made by the mother of St Thomas of Canterbury, and she said it before giving birth; and a woman who says it will never die in childbirth*

Lord God, almighty king,
Without end and without beginning,
Who deigned to descend to earth
And take flesh from the Virgin,
In order to save sinners
And deliver them from pain,
And you were born after nine months
Exactly, neither more nor less,
Circumcised and baptised,
According to your will,
Then offered as infant in the temple
And brought to God,
And you let yourself be laid in the cradle,
You, whom all the world cannot contain,
And drank milk from the breast
Of the holy virgin,
And all this you did for us,
True and glorious son of God;
By the great humility
Of your incarnation as man,
Listen to my prayer.
Jesus, true saviour of the world,
I am in danger of death,
Woeful and comfortless,
If I do not have your help
I have no hope of survival,
So I beseech you, true father,
For the love of your gentle mother,
Alleviate my harsh pain,
And grant that I may bear the child

I am carrying as pleases you,
And bring it to holy church
To receive the holy law,
That it be not struck down by death or hatred,
That it never suffer loss of vital limb,
That the devil assail neither it nor me.
Grant to me, son of Mary,
Escape from death, and span of life,
So that I may in your holy name
Accomplish my purification,
And serve you and holy church
According to the will and pleasure
Of your sweet mother.

Sweet maid, when the angel greeted you
The Holy Spirit cast its shadow over you;
For love of your son Jesus Christ,
Who took humanity within you,
Whom you suckled at your breast,
Look on me, your maidservant,
In mortal danger
If I do not have your help.
Merciful virgin mother,
I pray you, help me;
Holy maid full of pity,
Help me, so full of fear.

I beseech you, holy company of apostles,
Who in this life knew the fellowship
Of the son of God,
And beheld his miracles,
To pray for me
To Jesus, the true saviour.
And you, glorious confessors,
Who in the conduct of your lives
Were pleasing to God the king,
Appeal for me to our Lord God;
And you, precious martyrs,
Who often suffered anguish
For the love of Jesus the king,
Appeal for me to our Lord God;
Pray for me, holy virgins,
Who are all queens in heaven
With glorious Mary,
Through the chastity of your pure lives;
Pray for me to our advocate
Who has commended all of you,

Who has the whole world in his keeping,
That he will preserve me from harm;
All saints, both men and women,
Hear my sorrows and my laments;
Pray for me, all of you together,
To the sovereign almighty king,
So that he may keep death far away
And turn my suffering into solace,
And grant that my child
May appear in this world
Healthy and safe, to remain with us,
And let the devil never confound it.
Grant this to me, good Lord Jesus,
Physician of all ills;
Relieve my pain
And give me your grace.
Amen

## 20 Beatrice prayers

The prayer for Beatrice (**20.1**) and the prayer for peace and concord in marriage (**20.2**) formed part of the original manuscript. Neither prayer mentions Beatrice by name. The prayers for Beatrice after her death (**20.3**) were added in spaces originally left blank in the manuscript, or margins, and they name her repeatedly. All the prayers were probably variations on commonly used texts; other versions of **20.1** exist, and even the prayers for Beatrice after her death are full of rhetorical commonplaces, rather than personal in style and tone.

### 20.1 Prayer for Beatrice

*Deus qui liberasti Susannam*
Beatrice Hours
British Library Additional MS 33385, fol. 198r
Latin prose

Also in the DuBois Hours, Pierpont Morgan Library MS M.700, fol. 30r, as part of a commemoration to St Susannah, where Hawisia is named as suppliant (see **17.7** above).

God who liberated Susannah from false accusations, and Jonah from the belly of the whale, and Daniel from the lions' pit, and the three youths from the fiery furnace, and who stretched out your hand to Peter sinking in the water, deign to liberate me from this tribulation and distress, and from the power of all my enemies, and from all their confederates; because I do not know where to turn, except to you; because there is no other God who will help me except you alone, who live and reign in perfect trinity, God for ever, world without end. Amen

## 20.2 Prayer for peace and concord in marriage

*Deus pater pacem*
Beatrice Hours
British Library Additional MS 33385, fol. 198r
Latin prose

God the Father, establish peace and true concord and true love between my husband and myself, and give us peace on this day and on all the remaining days of our lives, so that we may rejoice in your peace, and the peace of Christ may abound in our hearts. You gave peace to Christ Jesus. Hear us, Lord, and grant us your peace in our days. Through Jesus Christ our Lord.

## 20.3 Prayers for Princess Beatrice deceased

*Omnipotens sempiterne deus cui numquam*
Beatrice Hours
British Library Additional MS 33385 (for fol. nos. see each text)
Latin prose

These short prayers were added very carefully to Princess Beatrice's book of hours after her death, at points in the manuscript where spaces had been left in the original compilation. This occurs, for instance, within the Little Office at the end of lauds (fol. 83v), and at the end of none (fol. 96v); at the end of the Hours of St John the Baptist (fol. 123v); and at the end of the Hours of St Katherine, following other additional prayers (fol. 140v).

While composed for Beatrice, the prayers evidently draw on the common formulaic stock of prayers for the dead. The requests for mercy and salvation of the deceased are couched in learned, often liturgical, terms, with rhetorical play on derivatives from the root *beat-* 'blessed, happy': linking the name *Beatrice* with beatitude and the blessed, especially on fols 123v–124r:

> *Beate* deus qui es gloria *beatorum* tue supplicamus *beatitudini* ut *Beatricis* ancille tue animam inter *beatos* beatificare digneris . . . Quesumus domine ut amore *beate* matris tue quam *beatam* dicunt omnes generaciones animam famule tue *Beatricis* associare digneris collegio *beatorum* . . . *Beata* spes mortalium deus qui solus post mortem *beatificas* animam famule tue *Beatricis* eterne *beatitudinis* premio *beatifica* cum *beatis*

1 fol. 23v
God of infinite mercy and immense majesty, be gracious, I beg, to the soul of your servant Beatrice, so that disencumbered of all sin

she may deserve to attain life, through our Lord Jesus Christ your son, who [lives and reigns] with you [ever world without end].

2 fol. 26r

Almighty everlasting God, to whom no prayer is uttered without hope of mercy, be gracious to the soul of your servant Beatrice, who departed this life confessing faith in your name; may she be numbered among your saints. Through our [Lord Jesus Christ your son].

3 fol. 40v

We beseech you, Lord, in your mercifulness, to have pity on the soul of your servant Beatrice, so that released from the contamination of mortality she may she be restored to the place of eternal salvation. Through our Lord Jesus Christ your son, who lives and reigns with you, God ever world without end. Amen

4 fol. 53v

We beseech you, almighty God, to release the soul of your servant Beatrice from every fetter of sin, so that restored to life she may breathe, in the glory of the Resurrection among your saints and chosen ones. Through Christ our Lord. Amen

5 fol. 83v

God, bestower of mercy and lover of human salvation, we beseech your mercy so that your servant Beatrice, who has departed from this world, may attain the fellowship of perpetual beatitude, through the intercession of blessed Mary ever-virgin, and all your saints. Through our Lord Jesus Christ your son, who lives and reigns with you and the Holy Spirit, God ever world without end. Amen

6 fol. 96v

God, to whom it is proper always to take pity and forgive, to whom no prayer is ever said without hope of mercy, in whose hands alone there is a remedy; be there at the moment after death, and be gracious to the soul of your servant Beatrice, so that released from the fetters of death she may deserve to attain life. Through our Lord [Jesus Christ].

We beseech you, almighty God, may the soul of your servant Beatrice be received by the angels of light, and led to the dwellings made ready for the blessed. Through our Lord Jesus Christ your son, who lives and reigns with you ever world without end. Amen. Amen. Amen

7 fol. 123v

Blessed God, glory of the blessed, we appeal to your blessedness to bless the soul of your servant Beatrice among the blessed, through our Lord [Jesus Christ your son].

We beseech you, Lord, by the love of your blessed mother whom all generations call blessed, to bring the soul of your servant Beatrice to the community of the blessed. Who live and reign with God the father.

8 fol. 124r

God, blessed hope of the mortal, sole source of blessing after death, bless the soul of your servant Beatrice with the reward of eternal beatification among the blessed. Through our Lord [Jesus Christ your son].

King of kings, Lord Jesus Christ, whom the sons of kings serve in honour, deign to place Beatrice, daughter of the king, upon a royal throne. Who live and reign with God the father.

Eternal king on high, who created your servant Beatrice from royal stock, we beseech you to let her be numbered among the sovereigns of your kingdom. Through our Lord Jesus Christ your son.

9 fol. 124v

To you, Lord, we commend the soul of your servant Beatrice, so that dead to the world she may live in you; wash away, through the forgiveness of your most merciful pity, whatever sins she committed through frailty of life in this world. Through our Lord [Jesus Christ your son].

[as in no. 3, fol. 40v] We beseech you, Lord, in your mercifulness to have pity on the soul of your servant Beatrice, so that released from the contamination of mortality she may she be restored to the place of eternal salvation. Through our [Lord Jesus Christ your son].

We beseech you, Lord, that the soul of your servant Beatrice may find the fellowship of eternal light, whose sacrament of perpetual mercy she has sought. Through our Lord [Jesus Christ your son].

10 fol. 140v

Almighty everlasting God to whom it is proper always to be merciful and to forgive, we pray and beg on behalf of your servant Beatrice, whom you have called from this world, that you should not deliver her into the hands of the enemy, nor forget her at the end; rather that you should let her be received by your angels and led home to paradise, and that she, whose hope was in you and who believed in you, should not suffer eternal torment but should have eternal joy. Through our Lord Jesus Christ your son.

God, life of the living, hope of the dying, salvation of all who hope in you, graciously grant that, with the intercession of Mary ever-virgin and all your saints, the soul of your servant Beatrice, released from the miseries of our mortality, may rejoice in perpetual light with your saints.

God, in whom all things have life, and the bodies of the dying do not perish but are transformed to a better state, we pray in supplication that you will let the soul of your servant Beatrice be received, led by the hands of your holy angels to the bosom of your beloved patriarch Abraham, and that in your pity and mercy on the last tremendous Day of Judgement you will wash away with forgiveness whatever sins she incurred through the treachery of the devil. Through our Lord [Jesus Christ your son].

## 21 Isabel Ruddok's prayer

*Domine deus omnipotens*
Isabel Ruddok's Hours
Bristol Public Library MS 14, fol. 46r–46v
Latin

It is unlikely that Isabel Ruddok formulated the Latin words of her prayer herself. Yet this does not mean that she did not *compose* her prayer; a helpful spiritual guide or cleric may well have written the Latin words along lines set out by her. There is a directness about the prayer, and some unorthodoxy, which make her own involvement very likely. She may well have been the source of the forthright repeated demands for victory over her enemies visible and invisible, and for divine intervention in confounding them. Moreover, it is striking that the first time she prays for liberation from sin, she includes a request to be liberated from troubles and perils and tribulations. The second time she prays for liberation from sin, at the very end, she shows forethought in asking rather unconventionally for all her sins, past, present and future, to be included. She cites the familiar biblical recipients of divine assistance – Susannah, Daniel, the three youths, Paul and Peter (see also texts **17.7** and **20.1**).

Lord God almighty, father and son and Holy Ghost, grant to me, your servant Isabel Ruddok, victory against all my enemies and antagonists, so they shall not be able to harm me, stand up against me or contradict me, but rather let their strength and counsel turn towards good, or come to naught. God, be my strength and my refuge and the shield of my defence, so that my enemies may be dispersed and confounded. God of Abraham, God of Isaac, God of Jacob, God of all who live well, free me, Isabel Ruddok, from all my sins and troubles and perils and tribulations; take away guilt, and give pleasant-sounding speech to my lips so that my words and my works may be pleasing to all who hear and see me. The prophet cries, the apostle affirms, that Christ saves those who trust in him; Christ helps, Christ redeems, Christ rules. May Christ ordain my triumph over all my enemies, and I shall not fear what man can do to me.

God, grant me salvation in your name, and in your mercy deliver me from the visible and invisible enemy. Lord Jesus Christ, son of God, who hung upon the Cross, and redeemed us with your precious blood, save me, Isabel Ruddok. As you liberated Susannah from false accusation, Daniel from the lions' den, the three youths, Shaedrach, Meshach and Abednego, from the flame of the fiery furnace, Paul from chains, and Peter in peril on the sea, so deign to liberate me, your servant Isabel Ruddok, from every evil deed, past, present or future. Amen

## 22 Elizabeth Scrope's precepts and prayers

Elizabeth Scrope's Hours
Cambridge University Library MS Dd.6.1

The manuscript was written in the fifteenth century; these prayers are added at the end, perhaps in Elizabeth Scrope's own hand; the handwriting looks similar to that of her signature (fol. 145r).

### 22.1 Moral precepts

*And ye will please God gretly*
Cambridge University Library MS Dd.6.1, 142v
Middle English verse
Ref.: *IMEV* and Suppl. no. 317
Ed. Person 1953, 25

There is some overlap with the recommendations of the learned Salernitan health remedies (see **27** below); a strictly moral life was held to be very valuable in promoting physical wellbeing.

If you will please God greatly,
Practise penance privately and discreetly,
And say your prayers devoutly and clearly;
Eat and drink in moderation,
Be watchful, pray and reflect;
Be serious, sober and chaste,
And do not waste any words;
Just as you love good meat and drink,
Attend to the quality of your speech and thoughts;
Love gentle Jesus fervently,
And take all adversity patiently,
And prosperity meekly,
And you shall attain heaven joyfully.
For under the sun a man may see,
This world is nothing but vanity;

Grace surpasses gold
And precious stone,
And God shall be God
When gold has gone.

### 22.2 Prayer in time of trouble

*O gloriosa, o optima, o sacratissima*
Elizabeth Scrope's Hours
CambridgeUniversity Library MS Dd.6.1, fol. 143r
English rubric, Latin prose text

This little prayer and its rubric demonstrate the suppliant's trust in Mary's power and mercy in times of need. The switch from 'whoever' to 'you' adds a personal note to the rubric, whereas the phrase 'your unworthy servant .N.' in the text shows that the invocation can be used by anyone. While the 'sinner' in the text is given in the feminine form, *peccatrix*, the 'unworthy servant' is masculine, *indigno famulo tuo*, which suggests that the text has been partially, but not completely, adapted for a woman's use.

*Whosum evyr is in any hevynesse*
*Whoever is in trouble, without counsel or comfort, should say the following prayer every day, and you will find help within a short space of time through the intercession of our blessed lady saint Mary*

O glorious, o best, o most holy virgin Mary, I, a wretched sinful woman destitute of all human help, beg your immeasurable clemency with all my heart, so that by the supreme joy the archangel saint Gabriel announced to you – that you were worthy to bear Christ the son of God in your holy womb – you will help me, your unworthy servant .N., in all the tribulations and perils of my soul and body, not according to my deserts but according to your great mercy. Amen

## 23 Alice de Reydon's prayers in tribulation

### 23.1 Prayer to Mary

*[D]uce dame gloriouse virgine seinte marie mere al seignur*
De Reydon Hours
Cambridge University Library MS D.4.17, fol. 77v
Anglo-Norman prose
No ref. found in Dean and Boulton 2000

Sweet lady, glorious virgin St Mary, mother of the Lord, I implore your guidance; as truly as the world was led astray by Eve and received good counsel through you, I beg you to pray to your dear son for me, so that for his gentle pity and immense mercy he may give me guidance in this matter for which I am appealing to you, with heavy heart, and deliver me from all evils, especially from this present anguish, and grant me his grace according to his pleasure, and a good span of life, and perfect repentance for my sins, and in this life such perseverance that I may end my life in his service and yours, sweetest lady, glorious virgin, St Mary. Amen

And say *Salve regina* 'Hail, queen' [as in text **1**, post-compline]

## 23.2 Prayer to God

*Ki est en tribulacion de cest siecle*

De Reydon Hours

Cambridge University Library MS D.4.17, fol. 78r

Anglo-Norman prose

This is a fifteenth-century addition to the manuscript, in a later hand than the additions on fols 75v–77v, from which texts **6.1**, **6.2**, **6.3**, **7.2**, **8**, **13**, **23.1** are taken

No ref. found in Dean and Boulton 2000

The rubric suggests that the suppliant finds herself in a place where she does not feel at home. The feminine forms 'she' and 'her' translate Anglo-Norman 'indefinite pronouns' which can apply to either sex.

*Whoever is in tribulation in this world, because of the place where she is, or through anguish of the heart, let her pray wholeheartedly and with good faith to God for deliverance, and have Masses sung as set out here, with the alms, and your prayer will be heard; but let the prayer be in accordance with God's will*

1 On Sunday have a Mass of the Trinity sung, and light three candles, and make an offering at Mass, and be in a standing position or on your knees for the duration of the Mass, and give three alms.

2 And on Monday have a Mass sung in honour of God and St Michael and all angels and all archangels, and light two candles, and make an offering, and make two charitable donations, and you should be standing or kneeling and offering at all Masses.

3 And on Tuesday have [Mass] of the Holy Spirit sung, and light seven candles and give seven charitable donations.

4 And on Wednesday have [Mass] of St John the Baptist sung, and of all patriarchs and prophets, and light four candles and make four charitable donations.

5 And on Thursday have [Mass] of St Peter sung, and all apostles, and light twelve candles and make twelve donations.

6 And on Friday have [Mass] of the Holy Cross sung, and light five candles and make five donations.

7 And on Saturday have [Mass] of Our Lady sung, and light one candle and make one donation with the other requirements aforesaid.

## 24 Princess Mary's prayer

*O mercyfull God, graunte me to covyt with an ardent mynde*
London British Library Additional MS 17012, fol. 192v
Middle English
Ed.: Maskell 1882, Vol. 3, pp. 287–88

The piety and learning of the eleven-year-old Princess Mary are attested by the rubric to this prayer, which names her as translator. St Thomas Aquinas (1225–74) was a member of the Dominican order, founded in Spain. There is likely to have been a strong Dominican influence at the court of Henry VIII during the years of his marriage to Mary's devout Spanish mother, Katherine of Aragon. The princess's education may well have been entrusted to a member of the order. 'Telling one's neighbour's faults' does not sound virtuous to a modern reader. However, it was one of the seven spiritual works of mercy (see **25**, and glossary entry 'Seven spiritual works of mercy').

*The prayer of St Thomas Aquinas, translated from Latin into English by the most excellent Princess Mary, daughter of the most high and mighty Prince and Princess, King Henry VIII and his wife Queen Katherine, in the year of our lord God 1527, and the eleventh year of her life*

O merciful God, grant me to long ardently for those things which may please you, to seek them wisely, to know them truly, and to fulfil them perfectly, to the praise and glory of your name. Order my life in such a way that I may do what you require of me; give me grace to know it, and will and power to accomplish it, and let me obtain whatever is best for my soul.
Good Lord, grant me a sure path that leads straight to you, so that I do not falter, in prosperity or adversity, but may give you thanks when I prosper and be patient in adversity, so that I am not borne aloft by the one or oppressed by the other; and let me rejoice only in what brings me nearer to you, and lament only those things which take me further from you; not desiring to please anybody, nor fearing to displease anybody, except you yourself. Lord, let all worldly things be loathsome to me, for your sake; and may everything that is yours be dear to me; and you, good Lord, most especially and above all. Let me be weary of any joy

apart from you, and let me desire nothing except you. Let all labour delight me that is done for you, and all repose weary me which is not in you. Make me lift up my heart to you often; and when I fall, make me reflect and repent, and steadfastly resolve to improve. My God, make me humble without hypocrisy, merry without shallowness, serious without mistrust, sober without dullness, fearful without despair, gentle without duplicity, trusting in you without presumption, telling my neighbours' faults without mocking, obedient without arguing, patient without grudging, and pure without corruption.
My most loving Lord and God, give me a watchful heart, so that no idle curiosity can draw me away from you. Let my heart be so strong that no unworthy affection can draw me backwards, so stable that no tribulation can break it, and so free that no coercion can challenge it. My Lord God, grant me wit to know you, diligence to seek you, wisdom to find you, conduct to please you, perseverance to look for you, and finally, hope to embrace you: to receive punishment in this life in your penance, and on my path to use your benefits by your grace; and in heaven, through your glory, to rejoice in your joys and rewards. Amen

## 25 Form of confession

*I knawe me gilty to God almyghty*
Bolton Hours
York Minster MS Additional 2, fols 1r–4r, 209r–210v
Fifteenth-century addition to manuscript made earlier in the century
Body of text, Middle English; with Latin headings
Refs: *IMEP* 6, 61–62; Jolliffe 1974, 70, C. 21 (this MS not listed)
Ed.: Barratt 2004

This form of confession is, for the most part, suitable for all lay men and women. It is a useful source of information regarding lay conduct and penance, as required by the church in late medieval times. However, there are incongruities (see Barratt 2004). It lists the seven spiritual works of mercy, and mentions but does not list the seven bodily works, such as caring for the poor and the sick, surely very familiar to the merchant class. In listing the sacraments it includes the only one which is reserved to the exclusively male priesthood: ordination in holy orders. In the section on the ten commandments (see the glossary for a more orthodox list), two attempts have been made to adapt the text for female use, each time with regard to sins of the flesh. Corrections made in the manuscript change the partner in sin from 'woman' to 'man', whether married or unmarried, related or unrelated, on one occasion; and the object of neighbourly desire from 'wife' to 'husband' on another (see footnotes). These changes demonstrate active female use of the Bolton Hours. There are two references to backbiting, as a branch of the sin of envy, and in connection with breaching of the ten commandments. The Susannah prayers found in several manuscripts attest the great fear their owners had of this particular vice (see **17.7**). The beginning of the same Form of confession is found as an additional item at the end of Isabel Ruddok's Hours (Bristol Public Library MS 14).

*Praise the Lord*

[*The seven deadly sins*]
*Pride*
I acknowledge myself guilty before God almighty and our lady St Mary and all the fair fellowship of heaven and before you, my spiritual father, earthly representative of God. Firstly, I acknowledge that I am guilty of the seven deadly sins: of pride of heart, disobedience to God and holy church, and, to the detriment of my soul's salvation, of proud speaking, incontinence in what I listen to, and in the clothes I wear, in possession of worldly goods, granted to me by fortune or family. Also in being ignorant of virtue, having no notion of good name, and hypocritically wanting to dissimulate and be commended by people more than I deserve. Wherever I have sinned in such manner or in any branch or ramification of this sin, I cry for mercy to almighty God.
*Anger*
I acknowledge also that I have sinned in anger of heart through my own presumptuousness, that is to say in rancour and hardheartedness, being contentious and striking my fellow Christians.
*Envy*
Also that I have sinned in envy, hatred, backbiting, slandering or defaming my fellow Christians, to bring them from good to ill repute, or I have cursed or harassed them so that I have not been in perfect love and charity. I cry for mercy to almighty God.
*Sloth*
Also that I have sinned through sloth, in opposition to the will of God and the salvation of my soul, that I have been heavy and dull and late in coming to God and holy church, and slow to begin any good work; and have not fulfilled in due time the penance assigned to me, as one ought to do, and have hindered God's divine service by chatting in holy church. I cry for mercy to almighty God.
*Avarice*
Also that I have sinned through covetousness, that I have not been content with the position and standing that God has decreed for me, but have coveted worldly distinction, more than one ought; that I have set my heart's desire on things that I have no right to, out of wrongful covetousness, and have wrongfully taken or withheld things, for which I cry for mercy to almighty God.

*Gluttony*

Also that I have sinned through gluttony many times, often consuming more food and drink than was reasonable for my bodily sustenance; at too late an hour, or too extensively, or too hastily; through which I have incurred sickness or disease, either in body or soul. I cry for mercy to my God.

*Lechery*

Also that I have committed the sin of lechery, in deed or desire, speaking foul words; also through embraces, kisses, and voluptuousness, that is to say, enjoying the rising of the flesh. Also that I have consented to the sin of lechery, to fulfil it in deed. I cry to God for mercy.

*The ten commandments*

Also, wherever I have broken the ten commandments, contrary to the will of God and the salvation of my soul, I cry to God for mercy. The first is that I have taken God's name in vain, in speech and idle talk, and I have sworn great oaths by his parts or members, and I have not loved God as one ought with all my heart and with all my will, nor made myself better able to please my God in word and deed. I cry to God for mercy.

Also, wherever I have not loved my fellow Christians as one ought and have not done unto them as I would like them to do unto me, in word and deed; also where I have been pleased when they fared badly, and sorry when they fared well. I cry to God for mercy.

Also, wherever I have not kept holy feastdays as I ought and have not come to God and holy church. I cry to God for mercy.

Also, wherever I have worshipped false gods or wrong beliefs or false idols or charms or images, or trusted in witchcraft. I cry to God for mercy.

Also, wherever my tongue has been given to backbiting against anybody, that is to say, in speaking ill of them, judging them unworthily and being more ready to speak evil than good; wherever I have enjoyed saying and hearing bad things. I cry to God for mercy.

Also, wherever I have sinned in the flesh with any \man/[2], whether married or unmarried, relative or no. I cry to God for mercy.

Also, wherever I have advised or abetted robbery or theft or the wrongful taking away of any person's goods against their will. I cry to God for mercy.

Also, wherever I have borne false witness against my fellow Christian by withholding evidence or swearing what is not true, which has caused them to lose trust, favour or good reputation, good name, goods or chattels or anything else, whether rightly or wrongly.

Also, wherever I have desired my neighbour's house, land, rents,

2 interlinear addition/correction, MS *woman*

tenements, or anything that cannot be lifted and raised up from the ground, that is to say, unmoveable things.

Also, wherever I have desired my neighbour's or fellow Christian's \husband/[3], or their maid or manservant or gold or silver or any other worldly riches, to which I have no right, so that I have done wrong in this way towards almighty God and my fellow Christian. I cry to God for mercy.

[*The seven sacraments*]

Also for the seven sacraments of holy church, that I have not observed honestly and purely as one ought, I cry to God for mercy.
That is to say, my baptism, that I received when I became a Christian, through which the original sin that I was filled with, and all other sins, were washed away. And that I have not maintained the faith and the pledge that I promised to my God.

Also, in the confirmation that I received from my spiritual father the bishop, to make me stronger and more stalwart in resisting the devil and his power, through being given the grace of the Holy Spirit, and to live a life pleasing to God.

The third sacrament that I have trespassed against is penance, that I have not fulfilled for my misdeeds with true contrition of heart, and frank oral confession, and satisfaction in deed, for which I cry to God for mercy.

The fourth sacrament that I have trespassed against is the holy sacrament of the altar [the Eucharist], consecrated by the priest and Christ's own words, which I have not received as I ought to, worthily and virtuously in purity of life, for which I cry to God for mercy.

The fifth sacrament that I have sinned against is the ordination of holy church, that I have received through the power of my bishop and have not observed in purity and chastity as one ought to do, for which I cry to God for mercy.

The sixth sacrament that I have trespassed against is matrimony, that I have not kept lawfully and justly as one ought to do for the worship and love of God and for the salvation of one's soul, for which I cry to God for mercy.

Also, the seventh sacrament of holy church that I have sinned against is extreme unction, that I have not heeded or been attentive to, as one ought, for which I cry to God for mercy.

[*The seven virtues*]

Also, regarding the seven virtues: that I have not observed and ruled my life in good temperance as one ought, that is to say, in meekness, righteousness, prudence, fortitude, and especially in the three principal virtues, that is, in faith, truth and charity. I cry to God for mercy.

3 interlinear addition/correction, MS *wife*

[*The articles of the faith*]

Also, regarding the articles of faith pertaining to the godhead and manhood of Christ: that I have erred in them, and have not believed in the godhead as one ought, and have not steadfastly believed in a true God who is father of heaven on high, and the son, and the Holy Ghost, three persons and one God, who is maker of heaven and earth and all creation. I cry to God for mercy. Likewise touching the manhood of Jesus Christ, how he was conceived of our lady St Mary and born of her, both God and man; also the Passion that he suffered for all mankind; and when his body was laid in the ground, his soul with the body and the godhead went to hell to save those that were lost; also on the third day following he rose from death to life, both God and man in one person; also forty days after that he ascended to heaven and sat at his father's right hand; also on Whit Sunday he sent wit and wisdom to earth to his disciples; also on the Day of Judgement he shall come to judge the wicked and the good who will then receive their just deserts. Inasmuch as I have erred and trespassed in these points, I cry to God for mercy.

[*The seven spiritual works of mercy*]

Also, that I have not performed the seven works of mercy, spiritual and bodily, towards my fellow Christians, such that in spiritual deeds I have not been merciful when people have trespassed against me, nor gladly forgiven them; and have not with reason reproved those who have done evil; and have not comforted those who have grieved, nor prayed for those who have sinned, nor given guidance to those who lacked comfort and counsel; nor informed or taught those who know less than I do, and have not been ready to instruct them. Our fellow Christians are much in need of these works, and the effects on them are wondrous.

## 26 Story-telling captions

*Ci vount les damoyseles au boys dedure*

Taymouth Hours

British Library, Yates Thompson MS 13, fols 60v–68r

Anglo-Norman prose (with one Middle English word, *wodewose* 'wild creature of the woods')

Refs: Brantley 2002; Brownrigg 1989; Dean and Boulton 2000, no. 248

These captions tell the story of the *bas-de-page* illustrations which accompany the opening of the Little Office in this manuscript. Commentators have been at pains to find a moral in the story, suggesting that it was designed to teach the book's young lady owner to excel in humility and gratitude: the young lady in the story should have remained humble, passive and grateful while an old knight despatches first the wild creature of the woods who was intent on ravishing her, and then a young knight who came upon the scene and desired her, as she him; as it is, she was guilty of unnatural ingratitude, unlike the old knight's hound who remained faithful to his master, and she was therefore abandoned by age and authority, and left a prey to a dismal fate. The young lady is finally portrayed kneeling in prayer as the old knight departs. In the so-called Smithfield Decretals, where a different series of pictures illustrates the same story, the young lady is seen at the end wringing her hands as she is attacked by two bears (British Library, Royal MS 10.E.4).

Such a depiction of a helpless and hapless female is unusual in these books of hours, where the predominant tone is more vigorous and optimistic (see the concluding remarks of the 'Interpretive essay').

1. Here the young ladies are going to enjoy themselves in the wood
2. Here comes the wild creature of the woods and carries off one of the young ladies as she is picking flowers
3. Here he is carrying the young lady in his arms
4. Here comes an old knight, Eneas, and rescues the young lady
5. Here the old knight leads the young lady by the hand
6. Here comes a young knight to claim the young lady
7. Here the old knight places the young lady midway between himself and the young knight
8. Here the young lady refuses the old knight, and goes to the young one
9. Here the young knight lays claim to the old knight's hound
10. Here the hound is placed beneath a tree mid way between the two knights, and the knights agree and proclaim that the one of them to whom the hound goes shall have him
11. Here the hound goes to his master, the old knight, and the young knight angrily vows to fight the old knight, and says he will have the hound as well as the young lady
12. Here the two knights fight, and the old knight kills the young knight
13. Here the old knight departs with his hound and leaves the young lady alone on account of her unnatural ingratitude

## 27 Salernitan recommendations for health

*Vinum latte lava oleum liquore fabarum*

Nuremberg Statdbibliothek MS Solger 4.4°, fols 229r–v

Latin verses

Early fifteenth-century addition to thirteenth-century manuscript

Refs: for comparable Latin texts with French translation, see Meaux Saint-Marc 1880; for Katherine de Valois and her family, see Hannagan 1991

These verses are in the learned, arcane, semi-alchemical tradition, with moral as well as medicinal theme. The recommendations, attributed to the renowned medical school of Salerno, include cheerfulness, work and moderate diet, as do the moral precepts in Elizabeth Scrope's Hours (**22.1**). Reference is also made to perilous days (see p. 8). There is much use of rhetorical figures of speech, balancing phrases and sounds, and alliteration. This makes translation difficult. For instance, the line 'From these comes balm, this is very true' is a weak rendering of *Ex hiis fit* ***salfa****, non est sentencia* ***falsa***.

The verses were added perhaps for the king of France, Charles VI, while the manuscript was in his possession. He suffered from poor mental health, and many of his numerous children were afflicted by poor bodily health. The manuscript was given by him to his daughter Katherine de Valois, queen of England, wife of Henry V and mother of Henry VI (see p. 16). Where the text is recommending a herbal concoction to improve eyesight, at line 3, there is an interesting marginal addition: *Pro clarificacione visus Regine* 'For clarification of the queen's eyesight.' Perhaps Katherine de Valois suffered from poor eyesight. Like most of her siblings, she was frail; one of the epidemics which afflicted the royal children may have damaged her eyes.

Douse wine with milk, and oil with bean juice,
Ink with wine; water purifies other things.
Fennel, rose vervein, celandine, rue –
From them comes water that restores sharp eyesight.
Garlic, fish fin, copper, fire, wind and scrap of smoke,
These things harm the eyes unless care is taken.
If you want to avoid heaviness let your meal be brief;
From a large meal comes huge pain in the stomach.
Sage, pepper, garlic, salt, parsley,
From these comes balm, this is very true.
Mint helps the stomach, sage the heart, rue the brain,
The liver enjoys charcoal, the spleen capers, the mouth locusts.
If after your meal you wish to dispel stomach-ache
Stand until you are tired, or walk a thousand steps.
Let the sick man have what he asks for, though not close at hand;
Nature is more vigorous when wishes are fulfilled.
In four ways ailments can be alleviated: through fasting,
Or sweating, or bloodletting, or potions.

The seventh of March is propitious, the eleventh of April hazardous,
Finally on the fourth of May, let as much blood as you please,
As long as you are not blind, or just recovering from fever,
And note that whoever is bled on the thirteenth day of February
Will not die in that year.
Summer and spring are propitious, autumn and winter hazardous.
If you have no doctors, let these three pertain:
A cheerful mind, work, and moderate diet.
Frequent anger, sorrow, busily pondering on many things:
These three waste away life, with no by-your-leave.
Leprosy, fever, itch, sore eyes, and falling sickness
Harm your bodies through contagion.
Truth always conquers falsehood in the end.

## 28 Herbal and other natural remedies

Beaufort Hours
British Library, MS Royal 2.A.18, fol. 2r
English

These sixteenth-century additions to the manuscript were made in different hands. The final assertion of the effectiveness of the migraine remedy, **28.2**, is added sideways in the top right-hand margin. The vernacular remedies tend more towards practical application than do the learned Latin Salernitan recommendations (see preceding text, **27**). The English remedies include instructions for making potions and lotions, where to procure the ingredients in one case (from the apothecary), how to use them, and for what purpose. An earlier text has referred to the benefits of prayer for clear wits: see the concluding section of the long rubric introducing the Fifteen Oes (**9.1**).

### 28.1 For healthy body, clear wits, memory, and prolongation of life

*Take rosemarie with the flowres*
Beaufort Hours
British Library, MS Royal 2.A.18, fol. 2r
English

Take rosemary with the flowers and distil the water from it. Make a sauce of it with sage, wood avens, marjoram, horseheal, cubeb, and a little saffron. Eat good food in moderation. Bathe in rosemary and wash your hands and face with rosemary water.
This renews the body and natural strength. It gives clear wits and augments memory; and when it is imbibed the rosemary gives more life to the body and helps natural functions and prolongs life.

In your milk [put] sugar, calamus aromaticus, lignum, aloes, cloves, and saffron.

### 28.2 Against migraine

*A different medson for the meigrem in the hede*
Beaufort Hours
British Library, MS Royal 2.A.18, fol. 2r
English

*A different medicine for migraine in the head*
For a man, take woman's breastmilk for a girl child; and for a woman take breastmilk for a boy child. Take three spoonfuls of the woman's milk, and as much running water. Then take stone of tartar – you can get it from the apothecary – and put a piece the size of a bean in the milk and water, and when it has dissolved take half a spoonful of the milk and water, and warm it bloodwarm on the fire. Let the sick person lie on a bed, and if their pain is all over the forehead, take half of the half-spoonful and let it drop in one ear and let them rest for an hour upon it, and at the hour's end, the same on the other side. And if the pain is on one side, put the drop in the other ear.
This medicine for migraine has been well proven; for those that have taken it three times have never had another attack.

## Interpretive Essay

## Women and their Books of Hours

This essay starts with observations on women's lives in England in the late Middle Ages. It goes on to consider their ownership of books of hours, their use of the books, and their possible participation in the writing of a few of the texts. Finally it returns to St Anne and the Virgin Mary.

Women's lives during the late Middle Ages were lived amidst violence and the constant threat of sudden death: from warfare, feuds, tyranny and persecution, or sickness. The hazards of childbed, infant mortality and the plague were never far away. There were wars between England and Scotland in the thirteenth and fourteenth centuries; there was the Hundred Years War between England and France from the mid-fourteenth to the mid-fifteenth century; there was civil war between the Houses of Lancaster and York in the second half of the fifteenth century. There were severe epidemics of the plague in 1349 (the Black Death) and in the early 1360s, and epidemics continued to occur. Noblemen conspired and rebelled against the king, often their kinsman, which resulted sometimes in their own deaths, and culminated four times in the death of a king, preceded in the first three instances by his deposition: Edward II was deposed and subsequently put to death in the third decade of the fourteenth century; Richard II at the very end of the century; Henry VI early in the second half of the fifteenth century; while Richard III died in battle in 1485. Richard III's short reign had begun with the death of his nephews, the princes in the Tower, in 1483.

Each usurpation or change in dynasty brought with it the imprisonment, exile or death of relatives and supporters of those who had fallen from power, and of rivals who were perceived to threaten the succession or legitimacy of the king of the moment. Women were sometimes pawns in these struggles. Occasionally they were very powerful themselves, as was true for some years of Isabel of France (1292–1358), wife of Edward II, and for many years of Margaret Beaufort (1443–1509), mother of Henry VII and grandmother of Henry VIII.[1] It was pre-eminently true, of course, in the sixteenth century of the

1 For the life of Margaret Beaufort see Jones and Underwood 1992.

half-sister queens Mary Tudor and Elizabeth I, daughters of Henry VIII.

Margaret Beaufort was noted among other things for her piety, as was her cousin Cicely duchess of York (1415–1495), mother of Edward IV and Richard III. Accounts have survived of both women's 'mixed lives' of secular responsibilities and prayer.[2] Of Margaret Beaufort we learn that she rose not long after 5 a.m. After 'certain devotions' she recited matins of the Little Office with one of her gentlewomen, and then matins of the day with her chaplain. She recited the Office of the Dead and Commendation of Souls every day. Before supper, she recited vespers of the day and of the Little Office, besides many other prayers and psalms of David. Before retiring for the night she spent at least a quarter of an hour on private devotions in her chapel. All of this could have been drawn from a book of hours, except for matins and vespers of the day, which were in the breviary. In addition she heard three or five Masses daily upon her knees, from the missal, while continuing with her own prayers and devotions, which again may well have been drawn from a book of hours. (She suffered from aching knees and back pain.[3])

We learn that Cicely duchess of York rose at 7 a.m. and recited privately with her chaplain matins of the day and matins of the Little Office. At the end of the day she recited with her chaplain vespers of the day and of the Little Office. The Office of the day would have been taken from the breviary, the Little Office from a book of hours. Mass was celebrated in her chamber before breakfast, and twice in her chapel during the morning, from the missal. At dinner there was public reading of a religious text, possibly from a book of hours, and the reading for the day was repeated after evensong at supper. During the afternoon there was an opportunity for private prayer and contemplation, for which a book of hours was probably used, though the duchess may have drawn on other sources as well.

Records of wills and other documents show that Margaret Beaufort and Cicely Neville owned significant numbers of secular as well as religious books.[4] An inventory of books belonging to Isabel of France made at the time of her death in 1358 suggests that she, too, owned and read a wide range of secular and religious literature in Latin and

[2] For Margaret Beaufort's religious practices, see Mayor 1876, 292–295; and Jones and Underwood 1992; for the piety of Cicely, duchess of York, see Armstrong 1983; for ample evidence of devout literate lay people pursuing the 'mixed life' of religion and the world in late fourteenth century England, see Carey 1987, 361.

[3] See Mayor 1876, 295.

[4] See for instance Meale 1996, especially pp. 140–44, 156 n. 79.

French.[5] Among the books found in her chamber were two books of hours, one large and one small. She bequeathed to her daughter Joan (1321–62) several Arthurian romances in French, and a book of Tristan and Isolda. Joan was married as a child to David Bruce king of Scotland, and it is possible that the early-fourteenth-century Taymouth Hours was made for her, perhaps as a wedding-gift from her mother, or from her sister-in-law Philippa, wife of Edward III.[6] The book will have accompanied her through decades of internecine dynastic and family conflict. Joan was destined to experience the deposition and death of her father Edward II, the violent death of her mother's lover Mortimer, her mother's decades of quasi-confinement at Castle Rising in Norfolk, the wars between her husband, King David of Scotland, and her brother Edward III, king of England, and her husband's defeat and years of imprisonment by her brother.

Katherine de Valois (1401–37), who received the Solger Hours as a present from her father a hundred years after it was made, was a royal princess of France and queen of England, like Joan's mother Isabel. One of only four of the twelve children of Charles VI of France and Isabel of Bavaria to survive into adulthood, she was married at the age of eighteen to Henry V of England.[7] Henry had first sought her hand six years earlier. Her elder sister, another Isabel, had been the child bride of Richard II, his second wife. She was sent home shortly before Richard was deposed by Henry V's father, Henry IV – an event which took place several years before Katherine was born. Katherine bore Henry V one son, whom the king never saw; the child was born at Windsor while the father was campaigning in France, where he sickened and died. Henry VI was crowned king of England, 6 November 1429, aged eight, and subsequently he was crowned king of France in Paris, 16 December 1431. However, Katherine's brother, the dauphin Charles, had already been crowned king of France, at Rheims, by Joan of Arc. Katherine, entirely loyal to her son, did not live to see him ousted from France by her brother's forces, and finally deposed from the throne of England, by his Yorkist rival Edward IV. The beautifully illuminated Hours of Katherine de Valois was made for her.[8]

5 See Cavanaugh 1980, 456–460.

6 Such books were a favourite wedding present. Queen Philippa paid Richard of Oxford for illuminating two small books of hours for her in 1331; see Ramsay 1987, 49–54; perhaps the Taymouth Hours was one of them.

7 For the life of Katherine de Valois see Hannagan 1991.

8 British Library Additional MS 65100; like many other beautifully illustrated books of hours dating from the fifteenth century, this one is remarkable for its illumination rather than for its texts, which do not extend far beyond the standard contents; there is, however,

*

A dozen more books of hours consulted for this study were made for royal patrons, or for women closely associated with a royal court; or they belonged at some point to royal households.[9] The Beatrice Hours was made for Princess Beatrice, daughter of King Henry III (reigned 1216–72). It was personalised as her own book by the prayers for her soul which were added after her death (**20.3**). Joan de Valence, daughter of William de Valence, half-brother of Henry III, was the patron of the Murthly Hours. Oxford, Bodleian Library MS Liturg. 104 passed at an early date in its history to a lady associated with the court of Edward III (reigned 1327–77). The Beaufort Hours, originally made for John Beaufort and Margaret Holland, and the Hours of Richard III, originally made for religious use in the early fifteenth century, were acquired by Margaret Beaufort. The Hours of Elizabeth the Queen, also originally made in the early fifteenth century, passed to Elizabeth of York (from whom it takes its name). Mary Queen of Scots, daughter of the king of Scotland and a great-granddaughter of Henry VII, is said to have been a subsequent owner of the Hours of Elizabeth the Queen, and to have given it to her attendant Dorothy Willoughby the night before her execution under Elizabeth I in 1587.[10]

A lady associated with the court of John duke of Bedford (1389–1435), brother of Henry V, first owned the book which subsequently became Eleanor Worcester's Hours. A lady associated with the court of Henry VII (reigned 1485–1509) was the patron of British Library Additional MS 17012, which contains 'autographs' of Henry VII and Henry VIII (reigned 1509–47), with requests to be remembered in the lady's prayers. Mary Tudor (1516–58; reigned 1553–58), daughter of Henry VIII and his first wife, Katharine of Aragon, was a subsequent owner of this book. Added to the manuscript is a prayer by Thomas Aquinas apparently translated into English by the eleven-year-old Princess Mary (text **24**). As an adult Mary Tudor also owned one of the loveliest late-medieval books, the Queen Mary Hours.

Recent research has brought to light valuable information about women book owners from nobility, gentry, and merchant classes.[11]

one interesting textual addition on fol. 26v: the opening stanza of a Marian lyric, *IMEV* no. 534 (*IMEV* does not list this manuscript).

9 The high proportion of royal books – approximately one-third of the total – may seem surprising. Backhouse lists 'sheriffs, constables, MPs' as the predominant patrons of books of hours (Backhouse 1975, 1–3).

10 See note in British Library catalogue.

11 See particularly Smith 2003 for the De Lisle, De Bois (spelt DuBois elsewhere in the present volume), and Neville of Hornby Hours; Cullum and Goldberg 2000 on successive merchant family owners of the Bolton Hours.

Books that were made for, or belonged to, women from the gentry or nobility in central or southern England include the De Vere Hours, the DuBois Hours, the De Mohun Hours, the De Reydon Hours, the Norwich Hours, the Carew-Poyntz Hours, the Tanfield-Neville Hours, and the Lyte Hours. Three important books from the fourteenth century, the Madresfield Hours, the Neville of Hornby Hours and the Percy Hours, originated in the north. Fifteenth-century merchant-class books are represented in this collection by three manuscripts: the Brotherton Hours, now in Leeds; the Bolton Hours from York; and the Hours of Isabel Ruddok of Bristol.

Textual evidence of female ownership, both in original contents and in subsequent additions, can be found in numerous manuscripts. The obit (note recording death) of Alice de Reydon, daughter of Robert de Reymes of Suffolk, was entered after her death in the calendar of her manuscript, the De Reydon Hours. The additions to the calendar of the fourteenth-century Tanfield-Neville Hours (text **4**) tell the story of women owners of the manuscript in the sixteenth century. Agnes Hykeley wrote her name in her book, and asked subsequent readers to pray for her (**9.3** headnote). The Lyte Hours has feminine forms in several prayers. That the Norwich Hours was intended for a woman's use, or at least was in a woman's possession by the time additional prayers were added, is attested by a feminine form *pecheresse* 'sinful woman' in an additional Anglo-Norman prayer to Jesus asking for help at the hour of death; and by the corresponding Latin form *peccatrice* in a prayer asking for mercy and intercession, and for the sacrament of confession at the hour of death (**7.1**, **14.2**). Isabel Ruddok's Hours includes as part of the original compilation her own prayer, with the phrase *Da michi Issabelle Ruddok famule tue victoriam contra inimicos meos* 'Give me Isabel Ruddok, your servant, victory over my enemies' (**21**), and there are several further references to her in the manuscript. The Brotherton Hours was made in Flanders for the English market; it has a prayer added in England, and adapted for female use in one verse (**9.2** 4 and headnote).

Elizabeth Scrope, Eleanor Worcester and Elizabeth of York, owner of the Hours of Elizabeth the Queen, all acquired their books of hours 'secondhand', and added their signatures. Eleanor Worcester affirmed her ownership further with a traditional bookplate text added at the end of the manuscript, perhaps also written in her own hand:

> And I yt los and yow yt fynd
> I pray yow hartely to be so kynd
> That yow wel take a letil payne

To se my boke brothe home ayayne
E. Worcester
(British Library MS Harley 1251, fol. 183v; *IMEV* no. 302)

In addition to the textual evidence of the obit in the calendar, further evidence of Alice de Reydon's patronage and ownership of her book is found in the heraldry, that is to say, in depictions of coats-of-arms. Illuminations combine the coat-of-arms of the family into which she was born with that of the family into which she married.[12] Eleanor de Mohun has been identified as the patron of the De Mohun Hours entirely on the basis of heraldry, which combines the De Mohun arms with the arms of Ralf de Willington, whom Eleanor married before 1337.[13]

The DuBois Hours and the Neville of Hornby Hours are outstandingly rich in evidence of female ownership, both through internal evidence of the texts and through their heraldry and donor portraits. The patron of the DuBois Hours is named as Hawisia in several prayers which are an integral part of the original compilation (see, for instance, **17.7**). The prayers by the Joys of Mary in this manuscript are very much women's prayers, dwelling on the joyful feelings of cradling and nursing (**12.1**–**12.3**). The book includes a fervent prayer for safety in childbirth, translated in the present volume from a copy in another manuscript, the Percy Hours (**19**). Entries in the DuBois calendar show that the manuscript passed from Hawisia DuBois, a laywoman, to her sister Maude, wife of William la Zouche de Haringworth, and then to the Audley-Giffard family in the fourteenth, and to the Welughby family in the fifteenth century.[14] In the DuBois Hours, its owner Hawisia is depicted in heraldic mantle with a male member of her family in full-page miniatures on fols 1v, 2r, and 3v. The Neville of Hornby Hours includes several specifically female prayers, and a rubric declaring the following prayer to be suitable for one in need of Mary's intercession during pregnancy (fol. 24r). Disappointingly, however, the prayer which follows on fols 24v–25r actually makes no mention of pregnancy, although the initial *P* is richly historiated with a picture of the Virgin Mary squirting milk from her breast towards a bare-breasted woman lying in bed. The book has portraits of the original owner,

12 Sandler 1986, Vol. 2, no. 67, pp. 75–76; at the beginning of the Little Office a female figure, presumably the patron Alice de Reydon, kneels below the Virgin Mary enthroned, with her child standing.

13 Michael 1982.

14 Smith 2003, Appendix 2; Appendix 3.

Isabel de Byron, and of her husband, son, and daughter or granddaughter.[15]

Many other portraits of patrons or 'donors' of books of hours are found, from the earliest manuscripts onwards; often the patrons are at prayer. In the De Brailes Hours the patron is painted four times in historiated initials: a fashionable, devout young woman, wearing a pink robe, red cloak and white hat, with hair flowing loose in the manner customary for unmarried young women at the time.[16] Further thirteenth-century, or very early fourteenth-century, books of hours in which women owners are portrayed include: the Egerton Hours, the Marston Hours, the Murthly Hours, the Solger Hours, the Vienna Hours, the Harley 928 Hours, and the Walters Hours.[17]

In the Taymouth Hours, a crowned female figure, probably the royal owner, appears three times. In the Beaufort Hours there is a donor portrait with Guardian Angel (fol. 26r). The donor holds a scroll inscribed *sub umbra alarum tuarum* 'beneath the protection of your wings'; the angel holds a scroll inscribed *dominus custodiat te ab omni malo* 'may the lord protect you from all evil' (see **18.1** headnote). In the Carew-Poyntz Hours, the Little Office has as 'frontispiece' a picture of a lady kneeling to receive the blessing of the child held by the Virgin Mary (fol. 86r). In the Bolton Hours there is a full-page miniature of St Zita with a woman, presumably the owner of the manuscript, kneeling in prayer before her, to one side (fol. 40v; see **17.6** headnote).

The patterns of book ownership could cross the boundaries between secular and religious communities, as could lay women themselves, especially in widowhood. The Tanfield-Neville Hours, originally a family manuscript, belonged in the early sixteenth century to an abbess, who in turn gave it to a newborn child as a baptismal gift (text **4**). Additions to the calendar of Eleanor Worcester's Hours include commemoration of St Bridget of Sweden (7 October) and the dedication of the church of Syon Abbey (20 October), which suggest that an owner of this manuscript – either Eleanor Worcester or a previous owner – had ties with the Bridgettine community of Syon Abbey. The Bolton Hours, though very much a merchant family book, as indicated by added inscriptions and calendar entries, also has marks of association with the Bridgettines. Among its numerous full-page miniatures are a portrait of St Bridget of Sweden, founder of the Bridgettine order, and, unusually, a full-page portrait of St Zita, to whom there is a prayer in the Syon

15 Smith 2003, 280; pl. 6; figs 87, 89, 91.

16 Donovan 1991, 23.

17 Donovan 1991, Appendix 3; Higgitt 2000, fig. 82, p. 118; pp. 182–183.

Abbey Hours (**17.6**). The Bolton Hours has a long sequence of graces before meals and blessings with manifold seasonal variations, surprising in a secular compilation. The original owner may perhaps have visited the Bridgettine community, in spite of the geographical distance between York and Syon Abbey at Isleworth, to the west of London. The merchant-class pilgrim Margery Kempe of Lynn in Norfolk records her detour to Syon Abbey to obtain a pardon, on her return from travels to Danzig and Germany,[18] which shows that links with the Bridgettines were not restricted to the nobility or gentry, or to those living in the vicinity of Syon (although the extent of Margery Kempe's mobility was highly unusual).

Several fourteenth- and fifteenth-century books of hours represented in this collection were actually made for nuns. The Amesbury Hours was made for the Fontevrault Benedictine nuns of Amesbury. Agnes Hykeley's Hours was made for a nun whose name is known but not her order; she signed her name at the bottom of a leaf and asked to be remembered in prayer by readers who might use her book when she was dead (**9.3**). The Malling Abbey Hours was made for Benedictine nuns, the Aldgate Abbey Hours for Franciscan nuns in London, and the Syon Abbey Hours for the Bridgettine nuns.[19] The Benedictine nuns of Shaftesbury owned Cambridge, Fitzwilliam Museum MS 2–1957. The Benedictines of Wherwell owned Cambridge, Fitzwilliam Museum MS McLean 45. The Dominican nuns of Dartford owned the manuscript that is now Taunton, Somerset County Record Office DD/SASC/1193/68, but it was not originally made for them.

From the information provided in David Bell's index of biblical and liturgical works in Latin owned by medieval English nuns, or nunneries, it is possible to deduce that female religious houses, or individuals in those houses, owned three types of book – books of hours, breviaries, and missals – in approximately equal proportions.[20] This suggests that the importance of the book of hours to these nunneries may have been as great as that of their formal service books, the breviary and missal. The prevailing view of the book of hours as a lay person's book may need to be revised, at least as far as women's books in England are concerned.[21]

18 Meech and Allen 1940, 245 n. 3.

19 The Syon Abbey community owned several more books of hours which survive in their own library, now on loan to Exeter University Library, and in the British Library.

20 Bell 1995, index IV, pp. 245–249.

21 Higgitt draws on several authorities for his statement that 'The book of hours is a class of prayer-book written to be used in private devotions by a member of the laity' (Higgitt 2000, 165); Gee states that very few surviving psalters and books of hours produced and

The small size of some of the manuscripts, both ones belonging to secular women and nuns' books, made them particularly suitable for carrying from home to church; they could easily be held in one hand, or attached to a belt or girdle. Two of the women's books of hours now in the British Library are very small: the Beatrice Hours, and Eleanor Worcester's Hours. The smallest of all in written space – 5.2 x 3.0 cm – is the Brotherton Hours now in Leeds University Library. However, this one would not have been easy to carry about because it is a remarkably fat little book, and would have needed a bag for safe conveyance. It makes up in number of leaves for the small area of written space per leaf, and the leaves are thick. The book that belonged to the nun Agnes Hykeley is another tiny book.[22] The very small books tend to have very large script, and rich illumination, encouraging their readers to dwell meditatively on pictures as well as words.

Donor portraits typically show the woman patron in private prayer to the Virgin Mary, sometimes in a homely setting, sometimes in the more formal setting of a chapel. A picture accompanying the Office of the Dead in Eleanor Worcester's Hours, by contrast, shows mourners with their books attending a church service, perhaps a requiem Mass. The books the mourners are holding are probably books of hours.[23] Rubrics giving instruction for prayer are frequently non-specific as to location, but sometimes they specify that the user of a book is to seek out a holy image, monastery or chapel. Levation prayers, to be said during Mass while the priest lifts up, or 'elevates', the body of Christ in form of bread, are a clear indication that a book of hours was designed to be taken to church.[24]

*

The rubrics of the Percy Hours are exceptionally informative regarding the various uses to which a book of hours could be put. These rubrics include 'performative' instructions for some of the prayers, which prescribe the location to be sought out when a prayer is to be recited, or the posture to be adopted during recitation, such as kneeling before the Cross, or lying prostrate on the ground. The rubrics show how the book was used for worship of the deity, and in prayers to Mary and her

illuminated in England during the reigns of Henry III and Edward I, Edward II and Edward III were originally commissioned by or for nuns, 'perhaps less than 10%' (Gee 2002, 38). The manuscripts reviewed for the present study suggest a figure closer to 20%.

22 Most nunnery books are rather larger, especially the ones with musical notation designed for communal use.

23 Littlehales 1897, xlv.

24 See texts **6.1**–**6.5**, and the conclusion of the Introduction, p. 23.

mother Anne, and to the apostles, martyrs, confessors and saints, most especially for individual penitential purposes – in preparation for death, and in the hope of attaining eternal life. Furthermore, it was used for all kinds of intercessory prayers, which ask for healing and for alleviation of a wide range of daily troubles. Great value is attached to prayers indulgenced by specific popes. The rubrics are considered here at length because they spell out most explicitly the wide range of uses and practical applications of prayers not only in this book, but also in numerous others. Implicitly, the range of uses will already have become apparent, through the survey of supplementary contents given in the Introduction, and, above all, through the texts themselves. Nevertheless, it is very useful to have them spelt out by a medieval compiler of such a book.

The Percy Hours was a family book, made for use by both men and women, with reference to the challenges of a man's life, such as battle, as well as to the challenges of a woman's life, such as childbirth. Yet it is also clear from the rubrics that even when the primary challenge was to the man, it might be up to the woman to recite a prayer on his behalf. They are usually written in Anglo-Norman French, but more learned Latin texts may be introduced by Latin rubrics and English texts added towards the end of the book may be introduced in English.

Following the standard contents, with their abundance of psalms in the Percy Hours, come recommendations for further supplementary recitation of psalms. The situations posited move from the general 'whoever has need of grace and help,' through unspecified anxiety, to what sounds like a heartfelt appeal for those who are 'afraid to go where they have to go' (fols 103r–106r).

Multiple recitation of psalms in front of the altar, presumably in the noble family's private chapel, is required in the event of engagement in battle, or another great enterprise (fols 110v, 117r). One of these prayers can be recited on another's behalf (fol. 110v), as can the prayer of St Brandan, which is introduced by an unusually lengthy rubric tabulating the immense value the prayer can have, when sung ten times kneeling or standing – perhaps on behalf of an absent loved one voyaging across the sea, who might not always be able to say his prayers – in terms of compensation for unattended Masses and unsung psalms and unspoken commendations of the dead (fol. 214v).[25]

Recitation of a single psalm will suffice for someone tempted to sin (fols 112v, 117v). However, mortal sin – of pride, wrath, envy, sloth,

[25] Legend had it that the Irish saint Brandan, or Brendan, eventually found the earthly paradise with sixty companions, after seven years of fruitless voyaging.

avarice, gluttony, lechery – requires serious action. The penitent must leave the family chapel, seek out the crucifix in a nearby monastery, and not let her eyes rise higher than the level of the feet of the crucified Christ as the prescribed prayer is recited (fol. 163r).

There is a prayer for help in unspecified times of trouble, for which the rubric prescribes a kneeling posture (fol. 107r). There are prayers to be said on getting out of bed, to see one safely through the day (fol. 107r). Prayers for special contingencies include one for success in litigation against a plaintiff or defendant more powerful than oneself (fol. 109v), and one for those going on a difficult journey (fol. 166v). There is one prayer, referred to as a 'brief' [= writ], which covers a wide range of dire situations. The rubric progresses from general dangers, for which simply seeing the brief will suffice, to specific perilous situations, where it is necessary to carry the brief on one's person (fol. 230r).

There are prayers for one suffering sorrow and anguish, both with and without the requirement to say the prayer at a specific time, Sunday, and in a specific place, before the blessed sacrament – that is to say, in the sacred place in chapel or church where the sacrament is 'reserved', or kept (fols 120v, 121v). It is good to recite the Five Pains of Jesus before the crucifix for remission of sin and salvation of the soul, though the inclusion of the phrase 'every day if possible' underlines the likelihood that at times it may not be possible (fol. 173v). There are prayers for warding off evil spirits and evil men, and for safe passage at the hour of death (fols 138v, 142r). There are papal indulgences, granting release from specified numbers of years to be spent in purgatory after death (fols 158r–v).

Prayers to the Virgin Mary will bring the greatest rewards imaginable, including safety in childbirth, and a vision of Mary before one's death. They will ward off all manner of ills, including ill-prepared death, that is to say, death without the sacraments of penance and extreme unction (fols 166r, 167r, 168r, 170r, 183r).

There are prayers for healing, and protection against evils injurious to health, in Anglo-Norman, and, in the later part of the manuscript, in English (fol. 176v, see **19**; fol. 194r). There are recipes in English for medicine to be used against colic and bad odours: 'for stinking breath that comes out of the stomach' (fol. 238r); and 'for stink that comes from the nose' (fol. 238v).

*

Given that women were active patrons, owners and users of books of hours, and sometimes wrote their names in their books or added marginal notes to them, the question arises as to whether they actually wrote any of the texts themselves, either in the sense of composing them or of putting quill or pen to parchment or paper. In the Percy Hours only the prayer for safety in childbirth is attributed explicitly to a woman writer – Thomas Becket's mother. The attribution only occurs in this manuscript, and may be a pious invention, designed to lend added authority to the text; yet it seems at least possible that this particular text really was written by a woman, whether or not she was Becket's mother.

The possibility of female authorship may be conceded also for the specifically feminine Anglo-Norman celebrations of the Joys of Mary in the DuBois Hours (especially **12.1**, **12.2**), and perhaps for the Middle English remedies for migraine and other ills (**28.1**, **28.2**) added to the Beaufort Hours, possibly during the period of Margaret Beaufort's ownership, who may perhaps have suffered from migraine as well as aching joints.[26] Princess Beatrice's Latin prayer for marital concord (**20.2**) and Isabel Ruddok's Latin prayer (**21**) may perhaps have incorporated or translated into Latin suggestions made to clerkly compilers of the manuscripts by the women owners themselves.

The English translation of the Latin *Gaude virgo mater Christi* is described by Anne Arundel as her sister Eleanor Percy's prayer, 'compiled' by her (**12.4**). There is evidence of a female translator – the eleven-year-old Princess Mary – in the rubric introducing the Middle English text of a Latin prayer attributed to St Thomas Aquinas (**24**).

Regarding scribal activity, the Pierpont Morgan Library in-house catalogue has a tantalising entry on page 6 of the description of the DuBois Hours, MS M.700: 'An increasing weakness of stroke and inconsistencies in usage of letter forms, especially in the d and in ligatures, raises the question of advancing age of the scribe or even the possibility that a woman may have written the text.'[27] Unfortunately, the discussion ends there.

Women's involvement in composing texts, or writing them out, is not attested in any of the numerous portraits of patrons in books of hours.[28] Nevertheless, the wider theme of women's literacy is represented in manuscript illumination, notably in images of St Anne and the Education of the Virgin. An example is reproduced from Elizabeth Scrope's Hours, plate 3, p. 113.[29] The image of St Anne teaching Mary

26 See p. 150 above.

27 Currently available at http://Corsair.morganlibrary.org

28 There is nothing in the books of hours to match, for instance, the images of Hildegard of Bingen or Christine de Pisan, pen in hand, in manuscripts of their works.

29 Scase 1993 and Smith 2003 have reproductions of further images of St Anne and the Education of the Virgin, and discussion; see also Wieck 1997, 13–14.

to read is sometimes taken to be indicative of women's role in teaching and learning in the late medieval family. This is supported particularly by those images in which Anne is teaching Mary to read from a book of hours, sometimes even from Mary's 'own text', the Little Office, and sometimes with the patron and further members of her family looking on.[30] The Bolton Hours has an ABC, suitable for first steps in learning to read – and also in learning to write.

*

In conclusion, notwithstanding the sombre tone of much of the Office of the Dead, the Penitential Psalms, the Hours of the Cross, sundry supplementary prayers, and the manifold images of Christ's Passion, the overall tone of the book of hours remains boldly affirmative, in line with the valiant woman of Proverbs and with the Gradual rather than the Penitential Psalms. The interweaving of the Office of the Cross and images of the Passion with the Little Office, so often found in English books of hours, adds depth and gravity but does not belie the book's confident tone of faith and hope. The two threads of intense sorrow and joy co-exist, in texts and images ranging from the divine and sublime to the human, humdrum and whimsical. Contemplation of the Passion of Christ and the Joys of Mary may be found alongside recipes for toothache and sketches of animals jumping over the moon.

For nuns and anchoresses books of hours would have been an important accessory to their service-books, breviaries and missals. For devout lay women they would have been the mainstay of their 'mixed life', a religious life lived not in a nunnery but in the world. The books surely offered at times an escape from the vicissitudes of daily life; in dwelling on the beautiful images, and reciting familiar prayers, their owners could find relief from everyday troubles. Yet, more than that, the books provided a foundation of prayer and contemplation in which life could be deeply rooted, offering solace to the truly penitent, comfort and remedies in times of sadness and affliction, and hope of salvation for oneself and one's friends and relations – the traditional Christian message, yet fortified by the life-giving power and energy of Mary and her mother Anne.

30 See particularly Cullum and Goldberg 2000; Smith 2003, especially pp. 259–264.

# Glossary
## of liturgical and technical terms, and proper names of importance to church history

**Aaron** Old Testament priest, brother of Moses, head of the house of Levi, whose rod budded and bloomed and bore almonds. Numbers 17, 3–8

**Abednego** One of three youths saved in the fiery furnace. Daniel 3

**Abraham** Old Testament patriarch

**Absolution** Remission of sins declared by a priest, following confession; culmination of the sacrament of penance

**Acrostic** Sequence of texts in which the first letters of each spell a word

**Acts of the Apostles** Biblical book of the New Testament which tells the story of Christ's followers and the early church in the years after the Crucifixion; traditionally ascribed to the evangelist St Luke

**Adam** The first man, according to the Old Testament creation story

**Advent** The period leading up to Christmas, beginning with the first of the four Sundays before Christmas

***Agnus dei*** 'Lamb of God'; phrase repeated three times during Mass in preparation for the Eucharist

**Alleluia** 'Praise Jehovah'; song of praise to God

**Alpha** First letter of the Greek alphabet; beginning of all things

**Ambrose** Latin father of the church (339–397), to whom the *Te deum* ('We praise thee, O God') is attributed

**Anchoress** A devout woman who has withdrawn from the world; sometimes but not always a member of a religious order

**Anglican** Of the Protestant Church of England, which broke away from the Roman Catholic Church in the sixteenth century

**Anglo-Norman** Form of French spoken and written in England in the late Middle Ages, after the Norman conquest of 1066

**Anne** (a) Mother of the Virgin Mary (apocryphal); feast-day 26 July; (b) New Testament prophetess Anna. Luke 2, 36–38

**Annunciation** The angel Gabriel's utterance to the Virgin Mary that she would conceive and bear Jesus Christ, the son of God. Luke 1, 26–38. Observed 25 March in the church calendar

**Anthem, antiphon** (a) Short liturgical text, often said or sung before and after a psalm; (b) Longer metrical prayer, often beginning a commemoration

**Apocryphal gospels** Accounts, especially of the infancy and post-Resurrection life of Christ and the Virgin, which are not part of the 'canon' included in the Bible

**Apollonia** Saint reputedly martyred in Alexandria in AD 249, during the general persecution of Christians; patron saint of those suffering from toothache; feast-day 9 February

**Apostles** Those sent to preach the gospel of Christ, especially his early followers

**Aquinas** See 'Thomas Aquinas'

**Archangel** Angel of the highest rank; in these texts, Gabriel and Michael

**Ascension** The taking up of Christ into heaven, commemorated ten days before Pentecost / Whit Sunday. Mark 16, 19; Luke 24, 51; Acts of the Apostles 1, 9–11

**Assumption** Taking up into heaven of the Virgin Mary, after her death or 'dormition'; commemorated 15 August

**Austin friar** Member of an order of friars which followed a rule based on the writings of St Augustine (354–430), one of the Latin fathers of the church

***Ave*** 'Hail'; the first word of the angel Gabriel spoken to Mary at the Annunciation. Luke 1, 28

***Ave Maria*** 'Hail Mary'; prayer to Mary recited by medieval Christians daily; recited at all hours of the Little Office, and on numerous other occasions; combining Gabriel's salutation to Mary with the words spoken by Elizabeth at the Visitation. Luke 1, 28 + Luke 1, 42

***Ave maris stella*** 'Hail star of the sea'; one of the major Marian anthems; sung at vespers

**Basan, Bashan** Fertile plateau east of the river Jordan

***bas-de-page*** Images, decoration and occasionally text added to a manuscript at the bottom of a leaf, below the lowest ruled line

**Becket** See 'Thomas Becket'

**Benedictine** Of the religious order of monks and nuns founded by St Benedict (c. 480–547), one of the Latin fathers of the church

**Benjamin** Youngest son of patriarch Jacob; one of the tribes of Israel was named after him; taken as the type of the much-loved youngest son

**Bestiary** Book describing animals, combining natural history with folklore and myth, often illustrated

**Bible** Scriptures of the Old and New Testaments; the former shared by Judaism and Christianity; the latter accepted as God's word only by Christians

**Book of hours** Book containing Offices prescribed for the canonical hours, especially the Little Office of the Blessed Virgin Mary; supplemented by further texts; for lay and religious use; often richly illustrated

**Brandan, Brendan** Irish saint (484–577) who, according to popular legend, sailed the seas in vain for seven years in search of the earthly paradise; eventually he set sail again with sixty companions and was successful

**Breviary** Book containing the Offices, or services, of the church recited daily at the canonical hours by people in religious orders

**Bridgettine** Of the religious order of monks and nuns founded by St Bridget of Sweden (c. 1302–73)

**Burial** The Burial of Christ, after the Crucifixion and Deposition. Matthew 27, 57–66; Mark 15, 42–47; Luke 23, 50–56; John 19, 38–42

**Calamus aromaticus** Aromatic medicinal herb; sweet flag, sweet rush

**Calendar** Table of months and days, with special notation of liturgical seasons, feast-days and saints' days; often expanded to include perilous days, and to record dates of local or individual interest

**Cana** Place in Galilee where Jesus performed his first public miracle, the turning of water into wine

**Candlemas** The blessing of candles for the whole year; a pre-Christian festival that coincides with the Christian feasts of Purification of Mary and Presentation of Christ, 2 February

**Canon** The biblical books accepted as the rule of faith

**Canonical Hours** Set times for prayer, with formal Offices, or services: matins, lauds, prime, terce, sext, none, vespers, compline

**Canticle** Non-metrical hymn or song from the Old or New Testament, used in the liturgy, e.g. Magnificat, Mary's song; often listed in medieval manuscripts as 'psalms'; from Latin *cantare* 'sing'

**Capitulum** Brief reading at the close of a service for the canonical hours

**Cedar, Kedar** Region east of Jerusalem and south-east of Damascus

**Cherubim** Small angels

**Christ** See 'Jesus Christ'

**Christmas** Festival of the Nativity of Christ; 25 December

**Christocentric** With central focus on Christ

**Christopher** Third-century Syrian saint and martyr, said to have been of huge stature and to have carried the Christ-child across a river; patron saint of travellers; invoked in books of hours in prayers for protection against the plague; feast-day 25 July

**Clerk** Man educated in the service of religion

**Collect** Prayer which 'collects' or gathers up prayers that have gone before

**Commemoration** Supplication to God or to a saint, typically comprising anthem, verse + response, and prayer

**Commendations** Prayers commending the dead or dying to the mercy of God

**Compassion** Sorrow at Christ's Passion suffered by the Virgin Mary

**Compline** The last service of the day, around 9 p.m., or sunset, completing the canonical hours

**Conception** (a) of Christ, at the Annunciation; celebrated 25 March; (b) of Mary, see 'Immaculate Conception'

**Confession** Acknowledgement of sin made to a priest as part of the sacrament of penance

**Contrition** Sorrow for sin committed; part of the sacrament of penance

**Co-redemptrix** Of the Virgin Mary: sharing in the redemption of mankind

**Coronation** The crowning of the Virgin Mary by Christ in heaven

**Creed** Declaration of religious belief

**Crucifixion** Death of Christ on the Cross. Matthew 27, 46; Mark 15, 24–37; Luke 23, 33–46; John 19, 25–27

**Cubeb** Pepper

**Daniel** (1) Young man miraculously preserved unharmed in the lions' den. Daniel 6, 16–23. (2) Book of the Old Testament

**David** Youngest son of Jesse; slayer, as a child, of the giant Goliath; later, mighty king; harpist, to whom the psalms of the Old Testament are attributed

**Day of Judgement** The day of final judgement on mankind, when men and women will be assigned to heaven or hell for eternity

**Deposition** The taking down of Christ's body from the Cross. Matthew 27, 57–58; Luke 23, 53; John 19, 38

**Devotions** Prayers in which the mind is given entirely to religious worship

***Dies Aegyptici*** See 'Egyptian days'

***Dies caniculares*** See 'Dog days'

**Diocese** District under the spiritual authority of a bishop; also under his legal authority, at least as far as matters pertaining to the medieval church were concerned

**Dissenter** Member of one of the Protestant groups, or sects, that broke away from the Anglican Church in the centuries following the Reformation of the sixteenth century

**Dissolution** Closing of the monasteries under Henry VIII in the sixteenth century

**Dog days** Latin *Dies caniculares*; the summer period when the Dog-star, Sirius, rises and sets with the sun; noted from ancient times as the hottest period of the year, most injurious to health

**Dogma** Doctrine asserted by the church

**Dominical letter** One of the first seven letters of the alphabet, used in calendars to calculate and mark Sundays throughout the year

**Dominican** Friar of the order of St Dominic (c. 1170–1221)

**Donor** Term used to denote the original patron, or owner, for whom a manuscript was made; especially in the phrase 'donor portrait'

**Dormition** The falling asleep, or death, of the Virgin Mary; celebrated particularly in the Eastern church

**Douay** Descriptive term used of one of the translations into modern English of the Latin text of the Vulgate; used in the Roman Catholic Church

**Easter** Major Christian festival celebrating the Resurrection of Christ on the Sunday after the Crucifixion (on Good Friday)

**Egyptian days** Latin *Dies Aegyptici*; dangerous days, often noted in a medieval calendar for each month separately, according to calculations thought to derive from ancient Egypt

**Elevation** The priest's lifting up of the body of Christ in form of bread, preparing celebration of the Eucharist

**Elizabeth** Cousin of Mary, and mother of John the Baptist. Luke 1, 36–61

**Eloi** 'My God'; first of Christ's last words on the Cross, 'My God, my God, why hast thou forsaken me?' Mark 15, 34

**Entombment** The placing of Christ's body in the tomb. Matthew 27, 59–60; Luke 23, 53; John 19, 42

**Epiphany** Church festival celebrating the coming of the Magi, or three kings, from the East; 6 January
**Epistle** Scriptural passage read before the gospel at Mass; typically from the New Testament letters of the apostle Paul
**Eucharist** Ritual consumption of bread transformed into the body of Christ; the sacrament of the Mass
**Evangelist** Author of a New Testament gospel: Matthew, Mark, Luke and John
**Eve** The first woman in the Old Testament creation story; tempted by the devil to eat the apple, against God's command. Genesis 3. Her Latin name *EVA* reversed in Mary's *AVE*, leading to the salvation of mankind
**Extreme unction** Sacramental anointing of a person with consecrated oil before death
**Fabliau** Popular tale, often with coarse ingredient, found in French and then in English literature from the thirteenth century; sometimes used in treatises and sermons for didactic purposes
**Feast-day** Day set aside for special reverence in the church calendar
**Flagellation** The whipping of Christ after his arrest in the garden of Gethsemane
**Flight into Egypt** Joseph and Mary's departure with the infant Jesus to Egypt, to escape persecution by King Herod. Matthew 2, 13–23
**Franciscan** Friar of the order of St Francis (1181/82–1226)
**Friar** Member of one of the late medieval religious orders who originally begged for a living; see 'Mendicant order'
**Gabriel** Archangel; angel of the Annunciation. Luke 1, 26–38
**Gathering** A number of leaves of a manuscript folded one within another, forming a unit for binding
**Gentile** In the Bible, anyone not a Jew; in some Christian writings, anyone not a Christian
**Goliath** Philistine giant of the Old Testament, killed by the young David
**Golden Legend** Celebrated collection of saints' lives by Jacobus de Voragine (1230–98); composed in Latin (*Legenda aurea* 'golden legend'), then translated into the vernaculars of western Europe
**Good Friday** Day on which the Crucifixion of Christ is commemorated
**Gospel** Narrative of the life of Christ; 'canonical' gospels are those by the four evangelists (Matthew, Mark, Luke, John) included in the New Testament; 'apocryphal' gospels are other narratives of the life of Christ
**Gradual Psalms** Fifteen psalms (Vulgate nos. 119–133, King James Bible nos. 120–134) often sung from the steps (*gradus*) of the altar; sung by the three-year-old Mary, one on each of the fifteen steps ascending to the temple, on the occasion of her Presentation, according to popular apocryphal legend
**Guardian Angel** Angel appointed to look after an individual's welfare, according to ancient pagan idea adopted by Judaism and Christianity
**Hagiography** Writing of saints' lives
**Harrowing of hell** Christ's descent into hell after the Crucifixion, and saving

of the souls of patriarchs and prophets – the righteous from the era of the Old Testament

**Heraldry** Display of signs typically painted on an escutcheon, or shield, by which an individual, a family or an institution was known; coats-of-arms

**Hermit** One who leads a solitary religious life

**Hermon** Sacred mountain in Lebanon

**Herod** (a) Herod the Great (c. 73–04 BC), king of Judea, from whom Joseph and Mary fled to Egypt with the baby Jesus; there is a difficulty with the dates (which suggest that Herod died before Jesus was born). (b) Herod Antipas (d. after AD 40), tetrarch of Galilee, under whom John the Baptist was beheaded and Jesus Christ was crucified; son or grandson of Herod the Great

**Historiated initial** Large initial at the beginning of a text in a medieval manuscript, often extending over several lines, decorated with ornaments and figures; sometimes containing a portrait

**Homily** Plain and practical sermon, as opposed to speculative, theological or doctrinal sermon

**Horseheal** Tall plant with yellow flowers; elecampane

**Hosanna** 'Save, we pray'; prayer for salvation, and praise, sung to Christ

**Hours** Religious service of anthems, hymns, prayers and readings sung or said at the canonical hours

**Hours of the Blessed Virgin** Hours with especial focus on Mary; core text of the book of hours; also known as 'Little Office'

**Hours of the Cross** Hours with especial focus on the Cross; often inter-woven in the book of hours with the Hours of the Blessed Virgin

**Hybrid** Half-human and half-animal figure sometimes found in manuscript ornamentation, especially in decoration of margins

**Hymn** Song of praise

**Idolatry** Excessive worship, of idols or of persons

**Illumination** Adornment of manuscripts with illustrations, decoration and coloured lettering

**Immaculate Conception** Anne's conception of Virgin Mary viewed as free from original sin and therefore 'immaculate'; celebrated 8 December; accepted by some from the Middle Ages onwards; accepted as dogma by the Roman Catholic Church only in 1854

**Incarnation** Christ's taking of human flesh

**Incipit** Opening words of a text

**Indulgence** Remission to repentant sinner of some or all of time due to be spent in purgatory after death; granted by a pope or bishop in return for performance of a set penance, prayers, or donations; sometimes attached to a specific deed, pilgrimage, or visit to a church or religious house

**Intercession** Prayer offered on behalf of individuals or communities by Christians; also by saints, especially Mary

**Introit** Anthem sung at the beginning of Mass

**Isaac** Old Testament patriarch, son of Abraham; offered as sacrifice by his father, but saved

**Jacob** Old Testament patriarch, son of Isaac, supplanter of his brother Esau in obtaining birthright

**Jerome** St (c. 342–420); one of the Latin fathers of the church, to whom the translation into Latin of the Bible (the Vulgate) is ascribed

**Jesus Christ** Founder of Christianity, born of the Virgin Mary at the beginning of the Christian era in Bethlehem, crucified on Good Friday c. 33 years later in Jerusalem (exact dates uncertain); believed by Christians to be the son of God, to have risen from the dead on Easter Sunday, and to have ascended into heaven forty days later, where he sits on the right hand of God and will assign all human beings to heaven or hell on the Day of Judgement

**Jerusalem** 'City of peace'; religious capital of Palestine, where Christ was crucified

**Jesse** Old Testament man of Bethlehem, father of David; the genealogy of Christ is traced from Jesse

**Joachim** Apocryphal father of the Virgin Mary

**John the Baptist** Cousin of Christ, who prophesied his coming and baptised him; executed under Herod Antipas

**John the Evangelist** Early follower of Christ; present at the Crucifixion; author of the gospel of John

**Jonah** Old Testament character swallowed by a whale, and delivered by God after three days and three nights in the whale's belly. Jonah 1, 17 – 2, 10

**Joseph** Husband of the Virgin Mary

**Joys of the Virgin** Five, seven, twelve, or fifteen joyful events in the life of the Virgin Mary; most frequently celebrated in late medieval England as: (1) Annunciation + Conception of Christ; (2) his Nativity; (3) the Resurrection; (4) the Ascension; (5) Assumption + Coronation of Mary in heaven

**Judah** One of the sons of the patriarch Jacob; one of the tribes of Israel was named after him

**Katherine** Saint and virgin martyr of Alexandria, Egypt, renowned for her learning, who allegedly declared her Christian beliefs and was beheaded in AD 307, after surviving torture on the 'Katherine wheel'; feast-day 25 November

**Lactation** Mary's feeding of Jesus with her milk (Lat. *lac* 'milk')

**Laity** People not in holy orders

**Lateran Council** General councils of the Western Church, held in 1123, 1139, 1179, 1215, 1512–17

**Lauds** Service at the canonical hour immediately following matins

**Lazarus** New Testament character raised from the dead by Christ. John 11, 39–44; 12, 1

**Lent** Forty-day period of fasting and penitence, beginning with Ash Wednesday and ending at Easter

**Levation prayers** Prayers to be recited during preparation for the Eucharist, while the priest is 'elevating', or lifting up, the body of Christ in form of bread

**Litany** Prayer of supplication to God, Mary, the apostles, confessors, martyrs, and all saints

**Little Office** = Hours of the Blessed Virgin Mary

**Liturgy** The rituals and prayers used in church services

**Longinus** Name given in apocryphal narratives to the soldier who pierced Christ's side with a lance (John 19, 34); in medieval drama Longinus is presented as a blind soldier, whose sight is restored when blood from Christ's wound touches his eyes

**Lord's Prayer** 'Our Father', prayer taught by Christ to his disciples; still used, often daily or several times a day, by Christians of all denominations. Matthew 6, 9–13

**Lucifer** 'Light-bearer', the brightest angel, who presumed to rival God, and therefore fell from heaven; Satan

**Luke** Author of the gospel of Luke, especially important for the book of hours because it contains the fullest account of the angel Gabriel's Annunciation to Mary, and of the Conception, Nativity and Presentation of Christ

**Magi** The three kings, or wise men, from the East, who followed the star to Bethlehem to worship the newborn Jesus

**Magnificat** New Testament canticle spoken by Mary; used in the Office at the canonical hour of vespers; still used in the evening services of the Roman Catholic and Anglican Churches. Luke 1, 46–55

**Margaret** Saint and virgin martyr of Antioch, allegedly beheaded after having been swallowed and disgorged by a dragon; patron saint of women in labour; feast-day 20 July

**Marian** Pertaining to the Virgin Mary

**Mariolatry** Excessive worship of the Virgin Mary, to the point of idolatry

**Mary** The Blessed Virgin Mary, mother of Jesus Christ. See especially Luke 1–2

**Mary Magdalen** Penitent sinner of the gospels; conflated in medieval narratives with other women in the gospels named Mary; possibly also with St Mary of Egypt, a penitent harlot of the early Christian era

**Mass** The most important church service, culminating in celebration of the sacrament of the Eucharist; requiring a priest as celebrant, it could not be performed by women alone, unlike the Office

**Matins** First of the canonical hours, usually sung or recited between midnight and daybreak

***Memoria*** = 'Commemoration'

**Mendicant order** Religious order of friars, whose members originally gained a living by begging; from Latin *mendicare* 'beg'

**Meshach** One of three youths saved in the fiery furnace. Daniel 3

**Methodist** Follower of the evangelical principles and practices of the eighteenth-century Anglicans John and Charles Wesley, who ultimately broke away from the Anglican Church to become Protestant 'Dissenters'

**Michael** Archangel revered also as saint; believed to have the task of saving souls from the devil on the Day of Judgement

**Miniature** Manuscript painting, often a portrait

**Missal** Book containing services for Mass throughout the year

**Nativity** (a) of Christ = Christmas Day, celebrated 25 December. Luke 2, 6–7; (b) of Mary, celebrated 8 September; apocryphal

**Nazareth** Home-town of Jesus and his family

**Nephthali** One of the sons of the patriarch Jacob; one of the tribes of Israel was named after him

**New Testament** Canonical books of the Christian Bible recounting the life and death of Jesus Christ, in the four gospels; containing also accounts of his followers and the early church, in the Acts of the Apostles, and some further writings of the apostles

**None** Canonical hour celebrated around 3 p.m.

**Nunc dimittis** 'Now let [your servant] depart [in peace]'; New Testament canticle; words spoken by the prophet and priest Simeon when he recognised the infant Christ as the saviour. Luke 2, 29–32

**Obit** Record of a death, sometimes entered in the calendar of a book of hours

**Office** The order or form of religious service recited or sung at the canonical hours, such as the Little Office or Hours of the Blessed Virgin Mary; unlike the Mass, the Office did not require a priest as celebrant, and could therefore be performed by the laity as well as by those ordained in holy orders, by women as well as men

**Old Testament** Canonical books of the Bible prior to the life of Christ; accepted by Jews and Christians as the Word of God

**Omega** Last letter of the Greek alphabet; conclusion of all things

**Ordained** Admitted to holy orders (possible only for men in the Middle Ages)

**Pagan** Pertaining to a community of the ancient world that was neither Jewish nor Christian, but whose beliefs or traditions might be incorporated into Christianity, as in the celebration of Candlemas or Easter

**Paraclete** Advocate, comforter; the Holy Ghost

**Passion** Sufferings of Christ, culminating in the Crucifixion

**Paternoster** 'Our father', from the Latin opening words of the Lord's Prayer

**Patriarch** An Old Testament 'father'; for instance, Abraham

**Patristic** Associated with the Latin fathers of the church, mainly of the fourth to sixth centuries of the Christian era

**Patron** Person who commissioned a manuscript

**Paul** Jewish rabbi who persecuted Christians; then converted to Christianity, and became one of the leading apostles and martyr saints of the early church; his bonds were miraculously loosed when he was imprisoned (Acts 16, 26)

**Penance** Sacrament through which absolution of sins is conveyed by a priest, comprising contrition, confession and 'satisfaction'; also, the satisfaction or atonement imposed by the priest

**Penitent** Suffering sorrow for sin; undergoing penance

**Penitential Psalms** Seven psalms, included in standard contents of the book of hours; recitation of these psalms often prescribed as 'satisfaction' within the sacrament of penance

**Pentecost** Feast celebrating the Holy Spirit's descent from heaven to the apostles at Whitsuntide. Acts of the Apostles 2, 1–4

**Pestilence** Plague; probably bubonic plague

**Peter** Leader amongst the early apostles of Christ, who tried to walk to Christ across the water, and was saved as he began to sink (Matthew 14, 29); saint and martyr; traditionally believed to have been the first bishop of Rome, hence the first pope

**Pharaoh** Title of the kings of Egypt

**Pilate** Pontius Pilate, Roman governor of Judea and Samaria who examined Jesus and delivered him to be crucified

**Polyphony** Musical composition with independent parts, or voices

**Presentation** (a) of Christ in the Temple, celebrated 2 February; coincides with the Purification of the Virgin; also known as Candlemas. Luke 2, 22–35. (b) of the Virgin, by her parents; celebrated 21 November; apocryphal

**Prime** Canonical hour celebrated around 6 a.m.

**Primer** Middle English term for book of hours, also spelt 'primmer', 'prymer'; sometimes differentiated (not in the present volume) to mean book of hours written in English rather than Latin, or book used to teach reading

**Protestant** Member of / relating to one of the churches that separated from the Roman Catholic Church at the Reformation, from the early sixteenth century

**Psalm** One of the psalms of David from the Old Testament; term often applied in the Middle Ages also to the canticles, including the Magnificat and Nunc dimittis drawn from the New Testament

**Psalter** Book containing the 150 psalms of David from the Old Testament; traditionally expanded in medieval England to include canticles drawn from the Old and New Testaments, Our father, Hail Mary, the creed, the 10 commandments, penitential prayers, articles of the faith, and further prayers; often with rich illustrations and musical notation

**Purgatory** Place in which souls are cleansed after death from pardonable sins committed during life on earth

**Purification** Cleansing of the Virgin Mary forty days after the birth of Jesus, according to Jewish ritual; celebrated 2 February; coincides with the Presentation of Christ in the temple; also known as Candlemas. Luke 2, 22

**Reformation** Early-sixteenth-century change of religion, whereby 'reforming' Protestants broke away from the Roman Catholic Church

**Response** Words responding to brief 'verse' that follows psalm, anthem or prayer in an Office

**Responsory** Response, as above, with elaborate musical setting

**Resurrection** Christ's arising from death. Matthew 28, 6–7; Mark 16, 6–7; Luke 24, 26; John 20, 14–17

**Rubrics** Words or letters written in red ink in a manuscript; usually titles or headings

**Sabaoth** Biblical word for 'armies'/'hosts'

**Sacrament** Sacred religious rite, comprising in the medieval church: baptism, confirmation, penance, Eucharist commemorating the Last Supper (= holy communion), holy orders (available only to men), marriage (not available to those in holy orders), extreme unction

**Salernitan** Pertaining to the renowned School of Medicine at Salerno, Italy

**Sarum** (Diocese of) Salisbury; according to whose custom, or Use, most English books of hours were compiled

**Satisfaction** Measures prescribed by a priest as atonement for sin within the sacrament of penance; often including recitation of penitential psalms

**Secular** Pertaining to the world rather than the church; of the laity

**Selmon** 'Shade'/'shadow'

**Seraphim** Six-winged angels of fire

**Seven deadly sins** Pride, anger, envy, sloth, avarice, gluttony, lechery

**Seven spiritual works of mercy** Converting the sinner; instructing the ignorant; counselling the doubtful; comforting the sorrowful; bearing wrongs patiently; forgiving injuries; praying for the living and the dead

**Sext** Canonical hour celebrated around noon

**Shaedrach** One of three youths saved in the fiery furnace. Daniel 3

**Simeon** Prophet and priest who recognised Christ at the Presentation, spoke the Nunc dimittis, and prophesied the sufferings of Christ and Mary. Luke 2, 25–27; 34–35

**Sina, Sinai** Mountain in the peninsula between the arms of the Red Sea from which God's Law was given to Moses

**Sion, Zion** One of the hills of Jerusalem, on which King David's palace was built

**Solomon** Great king, son of David

**Song of Songs, Song of Solomon** Poetic book of the Old Testament containing many images of love which came to be associated with the Virgin Mary

**Sorrows** (a) of Christ; his sufferings, culminating in the Passion and Crucifixion; (b) of the Virgin; at Christ's sufferings; renewed through his departure from the earth at the Ascension, until the time of her own death or 'dormition'

**Suppli(c)ant** One who utters a humble prayer asking for something, often for forgiveness of sins, or salvation

**Supplication** Earnest prayer or entreaty, as above; often in a litany

**Susannah** Old Testament heroine wrongfully accused of adultery, and cleared of the charge by a just judge (Daniel 13); merged in medieval accounts with various Christian saints of the same name

**Ten Commandments** The Christian shall observe the ten commandments of the Old Testament: there shall be no other gods; no graven images; no taking of the name of God in vain; the devout must remember the Sabbath; and honour their parents; they must not kill; nor commit adultery; nor steal; nor bear false witness; nor covet their neighbour's spouse, servants, or possessions. Exodus 20, 3–17

**Terce** Canonical hour celebrated around 9 a.m.

**Thomas Aquinas** St Thomas (1225–74), Italian theologian and Dominican friar of great repute; feast-day 7 March

**Thomas Becket** St Thomas Becket (1118–70), archbishop of Canterbury (1162–70); having been chancellor of England under Henry II, on becoming archbishop Becket became a champion of the church, and was finally martyred in his own cathedral; feast-day 29 December

**Theophilus** Early Christian bishop and beneficiary of one of the earliest Marian miracle stories; Theophilus signed a charter renouncing God for the devil, and the Virgin retrieved it for him from hell

**Tonsure** Shaving of the head, as on entering the priesthood or monastic order

**Trinity** The three-in-one God of Christianity: Father, Son, and Holy Ghost

**Ursula** Saint and virgin martyr; popularly believed to have been a British Christian princess who went to Rome accompanied by 11,000 virgins; all allegedly massacred at Cologne on the return journey, when Ursula refused to marry a local chieftain; feast-day 21 October

**Use** Customary arrangement of public church services of a diocese, e.g. Use of Sarum, Use of York

**Vernacular** Regional languages, e.g. English and French, as opposed to Latin

**Verse** Short prayer following psalm, anthem, or hymn

**Vespers** Canonical hour said or sung around 6 p.m.; the evening service, with Magnificat and other Marian prayers

**Visitation** Visit of Mary after the Annunciation, to her cousin Elizabeth who was pregnant with the future John the Baptist; celebrated 2 July. Luke 1, 39–56

**Vulgate** Latin translation of the Bible attributed to St Jerome

**Whitsuntide** Season culminating in Pentecost, the seventh Sunday after Easter, when the Holy Spirit descended to the apostles

**Wood avens** Herb with clove-like flavour; herb bennet

**Wycliffite** Associated with the church reformer and translator of the Bible John Wycliffe (c. 1329–84)

**Zabulon, Zebulon** One of the sons of the patriarch Jacob; one of the tribes of Israel was named after him

**Zacharias** Father of John the Baptist. Luke 1, 5–25

**Zita** Thirteenth-century Italian saint; a household servant from the age of 12, credited with numerous miracles; patron saint of servants; feast-day 27 April

# Annotated Bibliography

The bibliography gives full references for works cited, in addition to those already supplied in the list of abbreviations. The annotations give an indication only of a work's relevance to topics under discussion in the present volume.

The reader need not depend on printed sources for information about books of hours. There is an abundance of visual as well as textual material on the worldwide web, relating to books of hours in general and to individual books. The amount of information available on the web is rising very rapidly. A Google 'image' search for 'book of hours' yielded 100+ hits in June 2004; by June 2005 the yield had risen to 1000+.


Armstrong, C.A.J. 1942. 'The Piety of Cicely, Duchess of York: A Study in Late Mediaeval Culture'. In D. Woodruff, ed. *For Hilaire Belloc: Essays in Honour of his Seventy-Second Birthday*. London: Sheed and Ward, pp. 73–94.

Draws on a surviving household ordinance to depict the life of Cicely, duchess of York and mother of Edward IV and Richard III.

Ashley, K. and P. Sheingorn. 1990. *Interpreting Cultural Symbols: Saint Anne in Late Medieval Society*. Athens: University of Georgia Press.

Traces stories of St Anne, mother of Mary, from the second century A.D. through to the late Middle Ages.

Backhouse, J. 1975. *The Madresfield Hours: A Fourteenth-Century Manuscript in the Library of Earl Beauchamp*. Oxford: Roxburghe Club.

Facsimile of the original contents of this manuscript, excluding later additions; useful appendix with handlist of 24 books of hours made for English patrons, 1240–mid fourteenth century.

Backhouse, J. 1985. *Books of Hours*. London: British Library.

Authoritative general introduction to the book of hours, with illustrations.

Barratt, A., ed., 1992. *Women's Writing in Middle English*. London and New York: Longman.

This anthology of women's writing 1300–1530 includes texts from prayer-books and books of hours, with notes on texts and manuscripts.

Barratt, A. 2004. ' "Envoluped in Synne": The Bolton Hours and its Confessional Formula'. In R.F. Green and L.R. Mooney, eds, *Interstices. Studies in Late Middle English and Anglo-Latin Texts in Honour of A.G. Rigg*. Toronto: University of Toronto Press, pp. 1–14.

Edition of a Middle English form of confession from a York book of hours, with commentary and notes.

Bell, D.N. 1995. *What Nuns Read: Books and Libraries in Medieval English Nunneries*. Kalamazoo, Michigan: Cistercian Publications.

Three introductory essays are followed by a very useful inventory of manuscripts and printed books, including books of hours, listed alphabetically by location of medieval nunnery.

Bond, W.H. and C.U. Faye. 1962. *Supplement to the Census of Medieval and Renaissance Manuscripts in the United States and Canada.* New York: American Council of Learned Societies.

Includes description of De Mohun Hours and Lyte Hours.

Bradley, J.W. [c. 1900]. *Notes on the Lyte family book of hours.* London: Chiswick Press.

Interesting notes on texts, illumination and provenance of the Lyte Hours, with a few black-and-white reproductions of texts and images.

Brantley, J. 2002. 'Images of the Vernacular in the Taymouth Hours', *English Manuscript Studies*, 10, 83–113.

Investigates the conjunction of Latin, French and English texts in the Taymouth Hours, and the text-and-image combination.

Brown, C., ed., 1924. *Religious Lyrics of the Fourteenth Century.* Oxford: Clarendon Press.

Includes some Middle English texts which occur as supplementary items in books of hours.

Brown, C., ed., 1939. *Religious Lyrics of the Fifteenth Century.* Oxford: Clarendon Press.

Includes some Middle English texts which occur as supplementary items in books of hours.

Brownrigg, L. 1989. 'The Taymouth Hours', *English Manuscript Studies*, 1, 238–39.

Contributes to understanding of story-telling captions in the Taymouth Hours.

Bruylants, P. 1952. *Les Oraisons du Missel Romain.* 2 vols. Louvain: Centre de Documentation et d'Information Liturgiques.

Useful reference work for identifying prayers from the missal, which may occur in books of hours.

Camille, M. 1987. 'The Languages of Images in Medieval England'. In J. Alexander and P. Binski, eds. *The Age of Chivalry: Art in Plantagenet England 1200–1400.* London: Royal Academy of Arts in association with Weidenfeld & Nicolson, pp. 33–40.

Explores the balance of power between word and image in spiritual communication with God.

Carey, H.M. 1987. 'Devout Literate Laypeople and the Pursuit of the Mixed Life in Later Medieval England', *Journal of Religious History*, 14, 361–381.

Draws on devotional texts and inventories to demonstrate the importance of books in domestic devotion, especially for women.

Cavanaugh, S. 1980. 'A Study of Books Privately Owned in England: 1300–1450'. Diss. University of Pennsylvania.

Includes valuable information, derived largely from wills and inventories, on the ownership and transmission of books, including books of hours.

Cheney, C.R. 1997. *Handbook of Dates for Students of English History*, repr. Cambridge: Cambridge University Press.

Indispensable source of information on saints, popes, kings and calendars.

Clanchy, M. 2004. 'Images of Ladies with Prayer Books: What do they Signify?' In R.N. Swanson, ed., *The Church and the Book*. Studies in Church History, Vol. 38, pp. 106–122.

Considers the role of images in supporting reading, and aspiration to the divine.

Clayton, M. 1990. *The Cult of the Virgin Mary in Anglo-Saxon England*. Cambridge: Cambridge University Press.

Sets the scene for the development of Marian Offices and, ultimately, of the book of hours.

Cullum, P. and J. Goldberg. 2000. 'How Margaret Blackburn Taught her Daughters Reading'. In J. Wogan-Browne et al., eds, *Medieval Women: Texts and Contexts in Late Medieval Britain*. Turnhout: Brepols, pp. 217–236.

Examines evidence in the Bolton Hours of women's responsibilities in the family.

Dean, R.J. and M.B.M. Boulton. 2000. *Anglo-Norman Literature: A Guide to Texts and Manuscripts*. Anglo-Norman Text Society, Occasional Publications 3.

An indispensable source of information on supplementary Anglo-Norman texts in books of hours. Items are grouped by genre, and then listed alphabetically by incipit.

De Ricci, S. and W.J. Wilson. 1935–40. *Census of Medieval and Renaissance Manuscripts in the United States and Canada*. 3 vols. New York: American Council of Learned Societies.

Includes descriptions of DuBois Hours.

Donovan, C. 1991. *The de Brailes Hours: Shaping the Book of Hours in Thirteenth-Century Oxford*. London: The British Library.

This excellent study discusses the de Brailes Hours, and also has very useful appendices on texts and images in other thirteenth-century English books.

Dutton, A.M. 1995. 'Passing the Book: Testamentary Transmission of Religious Literature to and by Women in England 1350–1500'. In L. Smith and J. Taylor, eds. *Women, the Book and the Worldly*. Cambridge: D.S. Brewer, pp. 41–54.

Includes information about the transmission of books of hours.

Erler, M.C. 1999. 'Devotional Literature'. In L. Hellinga and J.B. Trapp, eds,

*The Cambridge History of the Book in Britain*. Vol. 3. 1400–1557. Cambridge: Cambridge University Press, pp. 495–525.

A rich source of information on both manuscript and printed books of hours.

Erler, M.C. 2000. 'The Abbess of Malling's Gift Manuscript (1520)'. In F. Riddy, ed. *Prestige, Authority and Power in Late Medieval Manuscripts and Texts*. York: York Medieval Press, and University of York, pp. 147–157.

An intriguing scholarly examination of local ties and power struggles in the transmission of the Tanfield-Neville Hours.

Erler, M.C. 2002. *Women, Reading, and Piety in Late Medieval England*. Cambridge: Cambridge University Press.

Examines the popularity of the book of hours with women readers, and gives new information regarding religious women's ownership of books.

Furnivall, F.J. 1868. 'The Nevile and Southwell Families of Mereworth in Kent, A.D. 1520–1575', *Notes and Queries*. 4th ser. 2, 577–78.

First scholarly note on the Tanfield-Neville Hours.

Gee, L.L. 2002. *Women, Art and Patronage from Henry III to Edward III. 1216–1377*. Woodbridge: Boydell.

Discusses patronage of the DuBois, Madresfield, De Mohun, De Reydon and Taymouth Hours. Gives full-page black-and-white reproductions from De Reydon and Taymouth.

Graef, H. 1963. *Mary: A History of Doctrine and Devotion*. London and New York: Sheed and Ward.

Still a standard work on Marian devotion.

Hannagan, W. 1991. 'Katherine de France, Reine d'Angleterre, 1401–1437', *Société d'Histoire & d'Archéologie de Senlis*. Comptes-Rendus et Mémoires. Années 1986–1987–1988–1989, pp. 39–80.

Full and sympathetic account of the life of Katherine de Valois, wife of Henry V.

Haraszti, I. 1955. 'Notable Purchases', *Boston Public Library Quarterly*, 7, 72–91.

Notes the acquisition by the Boston Public Library of the De Mohun Hours, and provides some details of the manuscript's contents.

Harthan, J. 1977. *Books of Hours and their Owners*. [London]: Thames and Hudson.

Still a standard work. Includes illustrations from and discussion of the Taymouth Hours.

Hicks, M.A. 1987. 'The Piety of Margaret Lady Hungerford', *Journal of Ecclesiastical History*, 38, 19–38.

Draws on inventories, furnishings, and texts, to convey a lively picture of a forceful woman, insistent on meekness and chastity in those dependent on her.

Higgitt, J. 2000. *The Murthly Hours: Devotion, Literacy and Luxury in Paris, England and the Gaelic West*. London: British Library and University of Toronto Press in association with the National Library of Scotland.

Masterly study of a woman's book of hours acquired by the National Library of Scotland in the late twentieth century, with CD facsimile and commentary.

*The Holy Bible*. Translated from the Latin Vulgate and diligently compared with other editions in divers languages (Douay, AD 1609; Rheims, AD 1582). London: R. & T. Washbourne (1914).

Version of the Bible frequently used by Roman Catholics for several centuries.

Hunt, T. 1990. *Popular Medicine in Thirteenth-Century England*. Cambridge: D.S. Brewer.

Examines the use of charms as well as orthodox Christian prayer in medieval medicine.

James, M.R. 1895. *A Descriptive Catalogue of the Manuscripts in the Fitzwilliam Museum*. Cambridge: Cambridge University Press.

Includes a full description of texts and 292 pictures in the Carew-Poyntz Hours.

James, M.R. 1924. *The Apocryphal New Testament*. Oxford: Clarendon Press.

Includes narratives of the infancy of Christ and of the Virgin Mary, and of the death of Mary, which yielded material for texts and, especially, for illuminations in book of hours.

Jolliffe, P.S. 1974. *A Check-List of Middle English Prose Writings of Spiritual Guidance*. Toronto: Pontifical Institute of Mediaeval Studies.

Includes reference to confessional texts as found in the Bolton Hours and Isabel Ruddok's Hours.

Jones, M.K. and M.G. Underwood. 1992. *The King's Mother: Lady Margaret Beaufort, Countess of Richmond and Derby*. Cambridge: Cambridge University Press.

Full account of the mother of Henry VII, and grandmother of Henry VIII, including her activities as translator and commissioner of printed books.

Kerr, B.M. 1999. *Religious Life for Women c. 1100–c. 1350: Fontevraud in England*. Oxford: Clarendon Press.

Includes discussion of the Amesbury Hours.

King, P. 1996. 'Corpus Christi Plays and the "Bolton Hours": Tastes in Lay Piety and Patronage in Fifteenth-Century York', *Medieval English Theatre*, 18, 49–62.

Classes the Bolton Hours as an English variant on a type produced in Flanders for the English market.

Lasko, P. and N. Morgan, eds, 1973. *Medieval Art in East Anglia 1300–1520*. Exhibition catalogue for Norwich Castle Museum. Norwich: Jarrold & Sons.

Includes useful accounts of illustrations and provenance of the De Reydon and Norwich Hours.

Lee, P. 2000. *Nunneries, Learning and Spirituality in Late Medieval English Society: The Dominican Priory of Dartford*. York: York Medieval Press.

A comprehensive account of flourishing devotional life in the only English convent of Dominican nuns.

Legge, M.D. 1963. *Anglo-Norman Literature and its Background.* Oxford: Clarendon Press.

Includes accounts of saints' lives, which are sometimes included in books of hours.

Littlehales, H., ed., 1895. *The Prymer or Lay Folks' Prayer Book.* EETS O.S. 105; 1897. Part 2. EETS O.S. 109.

Edition of a primer, or book of hours, in English, with an important essay by E. Bishop, 'The Origin of the Prymer' in Part 2.

Maskell, W. 1882. *Monumenta Ritualia Ecclesiae Anglicanae, or Occasional Offices of the Church of England According to the Ancient Use of Salisbury, the Prymer in English and Other Prayers and Forms with Dissertations and Notes*. 3 vols. Oxford: Clarendon Press.

These volumes include a primer, or book of hours, in English; Middle English versions of Latin prayers sometimes found as accessory texts in books of hours; also a service for the consecration of nuns.

Mayor, J.E.B., ed., 1876. *The English Works of John Fisher.* EETS E.S. 27.

Includes a remembrance of Lady Margaret Beaufort, delivered one month after her death.

Meale, C.M. 1996. ' ". . . alle the bokes that I haue of latyn, englisch, and frensch": Laywomen and their Books in Late Medieval England'. In C. Meale, ed., *Women and Literature in Britain 1150–1500*, Cambridge: Cambridge University Press pp. 128–158.

Includes discussion of some noblewomen's ownership of books of hours.

Meaux Saint-Marc, C. 1880. *Regimen sanitatis Salernitanum.* Paris: Baillière et fils.

An edition of the Salernitan recommendations for health, with modern French translation.

Meech, S.B. and H.E. Allen, eds, 1940. *The Book of Margery Kempe.* EETS O.S. 212.

The first full edition of this Middle English book, with very useful notes.

Meersseman, G.G. 1958–60. *Der Hymnos Akathistos im Abendland.* Vol. 1. *Akathistos-Akoluthie und Grusshymnen*, Vol. 2. *Grusspsalter, Grussorationen und Litaneien. Spicilegium Friburgense*, 2–3. Fribourg Helv.: University of Fribourg Press.

Authoritative collection of Marian hymns, salutations and litanies, with commentary.

Metz, R. 1954. *La consécration des vierges dans l'Eglise romaine.* Paris: Presses Universitaires de France.

Learned study of consecration rituals for nuns, drawing attention to the impact of these rituals in terms of drama.

Michael, M.A. 1982. 'The Hours of Eleanor de Mohun: a note on the coats of arms found in Boston Public Library MS 1546' [now 124], *The Coat of Arms*, New Series 5, no. 121, 20–23.

Expert identification of the patron of the De Mohun Hours, on the basis of coats of arms found at the beginning of every important textual division in the manuscript.

Miskimin, A., ed., 1969. *Susannah: An Alliterative Poem of the Fourteenth Century*. New Haven: Yale University Press.

Edition and discussion of popular Middle English version of the tale of Susannah, chaste wife of the Old Testament.

Morgan, N.J. 1982–88. *Early Gothic Manuscripts, 1, 1190–1250; 2, 1250–85*. A Survey of Manuscripts Illuminated in the British Isles 4. 2 vols. London: Harvey Miller.

Includes full description of the De Brailes Hours. Also has a very useful glossary.

Morgan, N.J. 1991. 'Texts and Images of Marian Devotion in Thirteenth-Century England'. In W.M. Ormrod, ed., *England in the Thirteenth Century: Proceedings of the 1989 Harlaxton Symposium*. Stamford: Paul Watkins, pp. 69–103.

Presents a wide range of complex material, with copious notes; adds substantially to understanding of texts and images in books of hours; translates some of the key texts.

Morgan, N.J. 1993. 'Texts and Images of Marian Devotion in Fourteenth-Century England'. In N. Rogers, ed., *England in the Fourteenth Century: Proceedings of the 1991 Harlaxton Symposium*. Stamford: Paul Watkins, pp. 34–57.

Continues the work begun in the preceding article.

Penketh, S. 1996. 'Women and Books of Hours'. In L. Smith and J. Taylor, eds, 1996. *Women and the Book: Assessing the Visual Evidence*. London, the British Library, pp. 266–281.

Examines women's portraits in books of hours for evidence of patronage and active participation in worship.

Person, H.A., ed., 1953. *Cambridge Middle English Lyrics*. Seattle: University of Washington Press.

Includes bookplate verse from Elizabeth Scrope's Hours.

Pfaff, R.W. 1970. *New Liturgical Feasts in Later Medieval England*. Oxford: Clarendon Press.

Includes discussion of the Compassion and Presentation of Mary, the Visitation, and the feast of St Anne, mother of Mary.

Procter, F. and C. Wordsworth. 1882–86. *Breviarium ad Usum Insignis Ecclesiae Sarum*. 3 vols. Cambridge: Cambridge University Press.

Includes Offices of the Virgin Mary in Latin, with seasonal variations.

Ramsay, N. 1987. 'Artists, Craftsmen and Design in England, 1200–1400'. In J. Alexander and P. Binski, eds. *The Age of Chivalry: Art in Plantagenet England 1200–1400*. London: Royal Academy of Arts in association with Weidenfeld & Nicolson, pp. 49–54.

Notes payment made by Queen Philippa in 1331 for the illumination of two small books of hours.

Reichl, K. 1973. *Religiöse Dichtung im englischen Hochmittelalter: Unter-*

*suchungen und Edition der Handschrift B.14.39 des Trinity College in Cambridge*. Münchener Universitäts-Schriften. Texte und Untersuchungen zur Englischen Philologie, ed. W. Clemen and H. Gneuss, Vol. 1. Munich: Wilhelm Fink.

Edition and discussion of an important miscellany of religious poems. Some of the items occur also in books of hours.

Revell, P. 1975. *Fifteenth Century English Prayers and Meditations: A Descriptive List of Manuscripts in the British Library*. New York: Garland.

Includes some prayers found in books of hours.

Roper, S.E. 1993. *Medieval English Benedictine Liturgy: Studies in the Formation, Structure and Content of the Monastic Votive Office, c. 950–1540*. New York & London: Garland.

Sets Marian Offices very usefully within the framework of monastic and popular devotions.

Saenger, P. 1985. 'Books of Hours and the Reading Habits of the Later Middle Ages', *Scrittura e Civiltá*, 9, 239–269.

Examines the spread of the book of hours and an accompanying new phenomenon: the fusion of prayer with silent devotion.

Sahlin, C.L. 2001. *Birgitta of Sweden and the Voice of Prophecy*. Woodbridge: Boydell.

Useful study of St Bridget, founder of the Bridgettine order.

Sandler, L.F. 1986. *Gothic Manuscripts 1285–1385*. Survey of Manuscripts Illuminated in the British Isles, 5. 2 vols. London: Harvey Miller.

An invaluable source of visual material, and commentary on texts and provenance as well as illustrations, covering the most innovative period of English books of hours.

Saupe, K. 1998. *Middle English Marian Lyrics*. TEAMS. Michigan: Western Michigan University.

Includes some texts found among the supplementary contents of books of hours.

Scase, W. 1993. 'St Anne and the Education of the Virgin: Literary and Artistic Traditions and their Implications'. In N. Rogers, ed., *England in the Fourteenth Century: Proceedings of the 1991 Harlaxton Symposium*. Stamford: Paul Watkins, pp. 81–96.

Looks at images of St Anne teaching the Virgin to read, several of which occur in books of hours.

Scott, K.L. 1996. *Later Gothic Manuscripts, 1390–1490*. Survey of Manuscripts Illuminated in the British Isles, 6. 2 vols. London: Harvey Miller.

Includes accounts of important fifteenth-century books of hours.

Seton, W.W., ed., 1914. 'The Rewle of Sustris Menouresses enclosid'. In *A Fifteenth-Century Courtesy Book*, ed. R.W. Chambers, *and Two Fifteenth-Century Franciscan Rules*, ed. W.W. Seton, EETS O.S. 148.

Gives the rule of life for a Franciscan nun, providing for private as well as communal prayer, with especial attention to the Little Office.

Simmons, E. 1994. transl. from American by C. Scheel. *Les Heures de Nuremberg: Reproduction intégrale du calendrier et des images du manuscrit Solger 4.4 de la Stadtbibliothek de Nuremberg*. Paris: Les Editions du Cerf.

Reproduces Solger Hours calendar and illuminations; looks at evidence of a woman patron in the circle of Edmund of Lancaster, brother of Edward I.

Smith, K. 2003. *Art, Identity and Devotion in Fourteenth-Century England: Three Women and their Books of Hours*. London and Toronto: The British Library and University of Toronto Press.

A detailed and very useful study of contents and provenance of the De Lisle, De Bois (DuBois in the present volume) and Neville of Hornby Hours, and further related manuscripts, with colour plates, and black-and-white reproductions and figures.

Stace, C., transl., 1998. *The Golden Legend: Selections / Jacobus de Voragine*. Selected and translated by C. Stace; with an introduction by R. Hamer. London: Penguin.

A useful modern selection of thirteenth-century tales; for the most part, saints' lives.

Sutton, A. & L. Visser-Fuchs. 1990. *The Hours of Richard III*. Stroud: Alan Sutton.

Detailed description of a very interesting early-fifteenth-century book of hours which came into the hands of Richard III, and passed after his death in 1485 to Lady Margaret Beaufort; with special attention to unusual additional devotions.

Waterton, E. 1879. *Pietas Mariana Britannica*. London: St Joseph's Catholic Library.

Still a good source of information on devotion to Mary, and on women's patronage of Marian relics, furnishings and shrines.

White, H.C. 1951. *Tudor Books of Private Devotion*. Madison: University of Wisconsin.

Traces the increasing popularity of the book of hours in late medieval England.

Wieck, R.S. 1988. *The Book of Hours in Medieval Art and Life*. London: Sotheby's Publications. Published as Time Sanctified: The Book of Hours in association with exhibition from collection of Walters Art Gallery, Baltimore. New York: Braziller.

A very informative collection of essays, covering both illustrations and texts. The sample includes four English books of hours. The appendix has standard and accessory texts and prayers in modern English translation.

Wieck, R.S. 1997. *Painted Prayers: The Book of Hours in Medieval and Renaissance Art*. New York: G. Braziller in association with the Pierpont Morgan Library.

Includes images of St Anne teaching the Virgin to read.

Wieck, R.S. 2001. 'The Book of Hours'. In T.J. Heffernan and E.A. Matter, eds, *The Liturgy of the Medieval Church*. Kalamazoo, Michigan: Medieval Institute Publications, Western Michigan University, pp. 473–513.

Excellent survey of the book of hours in the context of the medieval church as a whole.

Wilmart, A. 1932. *Auteurs spirituels et textes dévots du moyen âge latin*. Paris: Etudes Augustiniennes.

Still remains a standard work for many Marian prayers and other texts found in English and continental books of hours.

Wogan-Browne, J. 1996. ' "Clerc u lai, muïne u dame": Women and Anglo-Norman Hagiography in the Twelfth and Thirteenth Centuries'. In C. Meale, ed., *Women and Literature in Britain 1150–1500*, Cambridge: Cambridge University Press, pp. 61–85.

Offers comprehensive discussion and listings of Anglo-Norman saints' lives.

Yardley, A.B. 1990. 'The Marriage of Heaven and Earth: A Late Medieval Source of the *Consecratio virginum*', *Current Musicology* 45–47, 305–324.

Edition of the service for the consecration of a nun, preceded by discussion of its unique place in monastic ritual.

# Index

The index focuses mainly on medieval women and their books of hours, including especially the Marian component.

Most of the biblical proper names occurring in the texts (other than Mary, Mary Magdalen, and Susannah) are entered in the glossary rather than in the index.

Of the many kings of England mentioned in the introduction and interpretive essay, only Richard III is listed in the index. He is included because he owned a famous book of hours which may have been made originally for female use, whereas other kings are often mentioned only in order to identify their wives, mothers or daughters.

Numerical references in bold print are to texts, in normal print to page numbers.

Individual books of hours are indexed under **Books of hours**.

Books of hours from which the texts are drawn are followed immediately by a numerical reference in bold print. For further details of these manuscripts, see 'Manuscript Sources of Translated Texts', pp. 29–33.

**Already published titles in this series**

Christine de Pizan's Letter of Othea to Hector, *Jane Chance*, 1990

The Writings of Margaret of Oingt, Medieval Prioress and Mystic, *Renate Blumenfeld-Kosinski*, 1990

Saint Bride and her Book: Birgitta of Sweden's Revelations, *Julia Bolton Holloway*, 1992

The Memoirs of Helene Kottanner (1439–1440), *Maya Bijvoet Williamson*, 1998

The Writings of Teresa de Cartagena, *Dayle Seidenspinner-Núñez*, 1998

Julian of Norwich: *Revelations of Divine Love* and *The Motherhood of God*: an excerpt, *Frances Beer*, 1998

Hrotsvit of Gandersheim: A Florilegium of her Works, *Katharina M. Wilson*, 1998

Hildegard of Bingen: On Natural Philosophy and Medicine: Selections from *Cause et Cure, Margret Berger*, 1999

Women Saints' Lives in Old English Prose, *Leslie A. Donovan*, 1999

Angela of Foligno's Memorial, *Cristina Mazzoni*, 2000

The Letters of the Rožmberk Sisters, *John M. Klassen*, 2001

The Life of Saint Douceline, a Beguine of Provence, *Kathleen Garay and Madeleine Jeay*, 2001

Agnes Blannbekin, Viennese Beguine: Life and Revelations, *Ulrike Wiethaus*, 2002

Women of the *Gilte Legende*: A Selection of Middle English Saints Lives, *Larissa Tracy*, 2003

*The Book of Margery Kempe*: An Abridged Translation, *Liz Herbert McAvoy*, 2003

Mechthild of Magdeburg: Selections from *The Flowing Light of the Godhead, Elizabeth A. Andersen*, 2003

Guidance for Women in Twelfth-Century Convents, *Vera Morton with Jocelyn Wogan-Browne*, 2003

Goscelin of St Bertin: *The Book of Encouragement and Consolation [Liber Confortatorius], Monika Otter*, 2004

Anne of France: *Lessons for my Daughter*, *Sharon L. Jansen*, 2004

Late-Medieval German Women's Poetry: Secular and Religious Songs, *Albrecht Classen*, 2004

The Paston Women: Selected Letters, *Diane Watt*, 2004

The Vision of Christine de Pizan, Glenda McLeod and Charity Cannon Willard, 2005

Caritas Pirckheimer: A Journal of the Reformation Years, 1524-1528, *Paul A. McKenzie*, 2006

Women's Books of Hours in Medieval England, *Charity Scott-Stokes*, 2006

Old Norse Women's Poetry: The Voices of Female Skalds, *Sandra Ballif Straubhaar*, 2011

CPSIA information can be obtained at www.ICGtesting.com
Printed in the USA
LVOW01s2139090715

445649LV00023B/115/P

9 781843 843009